SHORT CUTS

INTRODUCTIONS TO FILM STUDIES

T0334794

FILM GENRE

FROM ICONOGRAPHY TO IDEOLOGY

BARRY KEITH GRANT

WALLFLOWER

LONDON and NEW YORK

A Wallflower Press Book
Published by
Columbia University Press
Publishers Since 1893
New York • Chichester, West Sussex
cup.columbia.edu

Wallflower Press® is a registered trademark of Columbia University Press

Cataloging-in-Publication Data is available from the Library of Congress

ISBN 978-1-904764-79-3 (pbk.)
ISBN 978-0-231-85006-3 (e-book)

Book and cover design: Rob Bowden Design
Cover image: *Blazing Saddles* (1974), Warner Bros.

CONTENTS

ACKNOWLEDGEMENTS

My deepest gratitude to Yoram Allon of Wallflower Press for inviting me to write this book, which for me has been a pleasure. At Wallflower Press, Jacqueline Downs capably guided the book through production, and my graduate student assistant Curtis Maloley worked on the filmography and index.

Some paragraphs are based on previously published material by the author: '"Man's Favorite Sport?': The Action Films of Kathryn Bigelow', in Yvonne Tasker (ed.) (2004) *Action and Adventure Cinema*, London and New York: Routledge, 371–85; 'Introduction: The Spokes of the Wheel', in Barry Keith Grant (ed.) (2002) *John Ford's Stagecoach*, New York and Cambridge: Cambridge University Press, 1–20; 'Strange Days: Race and Gender in Contemporary Hollywood Cinema', in Murray Pomerance (ed.) (2001) *Ladies and Gentlemen, Boys and Girls: Gender in Film at the End of the Twentieth Century*, Albany: SUNY Press, 185–9; 'The Classic Hollywood Musical and the Problem of Rock 'n' Roll', *Journal of Popular Film and Television*, 13, 4 (Winter 1986), 195–205.

For Genevieve again, who has tolerated too many violations of convention

INTRODUCTION

Put simply, genre movies are those commercial feature films which, through repetition and variation, tell familiar stories with familiar characters in familiar situations. Popular cinema is mostly comprised of genre movies – the kind of films most of us see, whether we 'go to the movies' or 'to the cinema', or watch films on DVD or videotape at home. Throughout film history genre movies have comprised the bulk of filmmaking practice, both in Hollywood and other national cinemas around the world. While there are different genres in different countries, the films that are made, distributed and exhibited in commercial venues everywhere are overwhelmingly genre movies.

Yet while genre movies are often understood as the equivalent of 'popular cinema', as opposed to art cinema and experimental cinema, the distinction is in fact hardly so clear. The films of such important yet diverse art cinema directors such as Jean-Luc Godard, Ingmar Bergman and Rainer Werner Fassbinder are infused with elements of genre. David Bordwell has argued convincingly that art cinema itself is a genre, with its own distinct conventions and modes of address, and that American genre films, as shown in the work of Robert Altman and Francis Ford Coppola, have absorbed them (see Bordwell 1979).

Popular cinema is organised almost entirely according to genre categories – science fiction, horror, thriller, pornography, romantic comedy, and so forth. From the particulars of film advertising in the various mass media to television broadcast schedules to the organisation of tapes and DVDs at the local video rental outlet, the idea of genre informs every aspect of popular cinema from production to consumption. The pervasive presence of genres in popular culture is clear when one considers that the word itself refers simultaneously to a particular mode of film production, often equated with the classic Hollywood studio system; a convenient consumer index, providing audiences with a sense of the kind of pleasures to be expected from a given film; and a critical concept, a tool for mapping out a taxonomy of popular film and for understanding the complex relationship between popular cinema and popular culture.

Tom Ryall has distinguished three levels at which we should understand genre in the cinema: the *generic system* (the relation of individual genres to each other and to Hollywood production in general), *individual genres* (defining individual genres and their common elements) and *individual films* (reading individual films within their generic contexts) (1998b: 329). This book will examine film genres and genre films at all three levels, focusing (although not exclusively) on American cinema, the most successful production centre of genre movies around the world. It offers a combination of theory and practical criticism, balancing ideas about genres with readings of specific films.

The series of case studies provide concrete examples of theoretical concepts and anchor them in specific texts. The films examined represent a range of genres across the history of sound film, and each discussion offers an analysis of the film as a genre film. Genre criticism allows for both the categorisation and evaluation of genre films. These are two very different critical tasks and should not be confused, although they often are. Genre helps us see the unique properties of individual works by permitting comparison of them with others that have similar qualities. As well, films, like all works of art, can only be judged in relation to other works.

Chapter 1 begins by placing film genres within the wider context of popular culture, itself comprised of numerous generic discourses in a variety of media. The emphasis of the chapter is on explaining the various elements of genre films, including conventions, iconography, settings, narratives, characters and actors. The chapter concludes with a consideration of the problems of genre definition, with film noir as a specific example. Chapter 2 examines how genre films relate to the culture that produces them. Genre films are discussed as mass-mediated equivalents to ritual and myth that address both topical issues arising at particular historical moments and more universal questions. Within these contexts, questions of ideology and history are explored in case studies of the musical and the horror genres. Chapter 3 explores issues of authorship in the context of genre, and includes several case studies of recognised auteurs showing how directors with different sensibilities are able to work within generic traditions to express their own vision. Chapter 4 considers broader questions of representation, focusing on how genre films depict gender, race, sexuality and class, again supported with several case studies. The book concludes by moving beyond Hollywood and American cinema to consider other national cinemas and their involvement in genre filmmaking.

Throughout, the aim has been to balance general claims with specific examples, and textual analysis with historical and cultural context. While theoretical approaches such as feminism, psychoanalysis, structuralism and postmodernism are employed, the emphasis here is on their accessibility and relevance for the study of film genre and genre films. Thus, this book is neither a genre history nor a history of genre theory and criticism, but rather a broad introduction to the topic that will provide the necessary tools and models for understanding and appreciating genre films.

1 APPROACHING FILM GENRE

Genre and Popular Culture

Although central to film, genres far exceed the cinema. As Rick Altman observes: 'Of all the concepts fundamental to literary theory, none has a longer and more distinguished lineage than the question of literary types or genres' (1999: 1). The western was already established in literature before the invention of cinema, while the musical took much from pre-existing theatre forms and conventions. Providing a useful overview of the historical debates surrounding literary genres, Altman argues that Aristotle, the first genre theorist, initiated the unfortunate tendency of genre analysis to restrict discussion to textual analysis. Nevertheless, in his *Poetics* Aristotle did address two major concerns of film genre study. First, in distinguishing between the very different kinds of endings in comedy and tragedy, Aristotle anticipated the descriptive attempts of film genre study to enumerate the formal properties of genres, the common elements that allow a number of films to be grouped together and conceived as a category. Second, Aristotle's notion that tragedy is achieved through a psychological affect (catharsis, the purgation of fear and pity aroused through identification with the actions of a tragic hero) prefigures the critical attention given to the ways in which genre films address spectators as well as the particular pleasures and experiences offered to viewers by different genres. Already Aristotle was considering the fundamental question of why people like genre works – a particularly thorny question given their formulaic, repetitive qualities.

Classical literary theory assumed differences between literature and popular writing; such judgements were based on underlying assumptions of aesthetic value. This distinction continued in the modern era as a debate between 'true' art and popular culture, art and trash, high-brow and low-brow. If good art was original, distinctive and complex, 'the best that has been thought and said', as Matthew Arnold put it (1960: 6), then popular art was formulaic and unsophisticated. Popular culture (including, of course, film) has often been criticised for lacking originality or authenticity. In the 1930s and 1940s, cultural theorists associated with the Frankfurt School's Institute for Social Research dismissed popular art as industrial products of a capitalist economy that inculcates false consciousness. Most influentially, Theodor Adorno and Max Horkheimer (1997) argued that popular culture – the culture industry, as they termed it – had turned folk art into commodities of mass culture, and that generic formulas functioned simply to control the masses of consumers by organising and labelling them like the films themselves. Later, in the United States, Dwight Macdonald argued that modern industrialisation had eroded the earlier distinction between high art and popular art, resulting in the rise of mass cult, which he derided as formulaic at every level (1964: 14). Traditional critical thinking consigned genre art in whatever form to the realm of the popular and, for the most part, excluded it from the canon.

Although such cultural distinctions are still upheld by many, high culture and popular culture in fact had merged long before Mickey Mouse shook hands with orchestra conductor Leopold Stokowski in Walt Disney's *Fantasia* (1940). In 1915 literary critic Van Wyck Brooks wrote about the split in American culture between high-brow and low-brow, and suggested there was 'no community, no genial middle ground' (1970: 18). But already he might have looked to the movies, where popular, formula-driven motion pictures were even then gathering large and faithful communities of spectators across the United States. Movies were central to the American ideal of the melting pot, for they were an inexpensive entertainment that introduced newly-arrived immigrants to the American way in visual stories that transcended the barrier of language.

Indeed, because of the importance of genre movies within culture, and because they are collaborative efforts that require the work of many individuals, genre movies have been commonly understood as inevitable expressions of the contemporary *zeitgeist*. This is true not only of individual genre movies, but also of the changing patterns and popularity of different genres and of the shifting relationships between them. For whether they are set in the past or in the future, on the mean streets of contemporary New York or long ago in a galaxy far away, genre movies are always about the time and place in which they are made.

Today, with entertainment in its myriad forms controlled by an increasingly small number of transnational corporations, popular culture is largely mass culture in the derogatory sense that Macdonald claimed. However, many politically-oriented critics understand the importance of studying popular culture, if for no other reason than to expose the ideology of its artefacts. But they also argue that works of popular culture offer empowerment to various cultural groups and are sites of ideological struggle rather than mere purveyors of the status quo. Taking a more inclusive view of cultural production and avoiding the value judgements of high-brow critics like Macdonald, John Cawelti suggests that all art be thought of as existing on a continuum between invention and convention (1985: 27–9). Such a perspective allows for a greater appreciation and understanding of genre texts and how they work.

Whatever their politics, genre movies are intimately imbricated within larger cultural discourses as well as political ones. As Steve Neale points out, within popular culture genres always exceed simply a group of films or other texts. Neale emphasises the importance of advertisements, publicity photos and studio stills, reviews and so on in keying and shaping viewers' expectations even before they see a film by promoting its 'generic image' (2003: 164). These instances of 'institutional' and 'industrial' discourse reveal how audiences perceived films when they were released, and also help us understand how genres have changed over time. As an example, Neale notes that most histories of the western film begin with *The Great Train Robbery* (1903), but when released it was promoted not as a western but marketed for its relation to the then-popular genres of the chase film, the railroad film and the crime film; at that time, there was no recognised genre known as the western into which to categorise it.

The Classic Studio System

Early filmmaking in the US was located in and around New York City on the east coast, near the nation's urban, industrial centres. But southern

California quickly proved more appealing, and film pioneer D. W. Griffith and many others moved west. The area around Los Angeles was attractive to film companies for a number of reasons. Geographically distant from the controlling power of the monopolistic Motion Pictures Patent Company, founded in the east in 1908, the region's more hospitable climate also offered more varied topography and provided greater opportunities for location shooting. Labour and land were also less expensive than in the east, and incoming film companies were able to buy large tracts on which to build their studios for interior shooting. Thus, the American film industry became concentrated in a relatively small area, Hollywood. Dubbed the 'dream factory' by anthropologist Hortense Powdermaker in 1950, Hollywood produced appealing fantasies in an industrial context that millions of people have watched, as if in dreams awake.

Regularised film exhibition developed as a result of the popularity and rapid growth of nickelodeons, the first venues devoted exclusively to cinema exhibition. The steady demand for new films made year-round production schedules necessary and provided the impetus for the development of a factory-based (Fordist) mode of production. As movies were made in a competitive, profit-motivated context, the Hollywood studios developed a production system that supplied 'product'. In the Studio Era (roughly 1920s–1950s), all members of the cast and crew were workers under contract to the studio, and the different kinds of work (for example, script, editing, music) were divided into departments. Very few directors were able to choose their own projects, but were required to direct movies as the studio heads and producers dictated.

Hollywood movies have become so dominant throughout the world that the terms 'Hollywood style' or 'classic narrative style' are often used interchangeably to refer to the style of narrative filmmaking that emphasises the crisp and seamless flow of the story combined with high production values. Film historians have argued convincingly for a view of Hollywood cinema as 'a distinct mode of film practice' with its origins dating as early as 1917 (Bordwell, Staiger & Thompson 1985: xiii). Within the context of Hollywood's industrial mode of production, genre movies are dependable products.

Genre filmmaking developed early, with producers seeking maximum acceptance at the box office through the repetition and variation of commercially successful formulas. Seeking to balance standardisation and differentiation, filmmakers combined sameness and difference. The formulaic qualities of genre films meant that studios could turn them out quickly, and audiences could understand them just as quickly. In their catalogues, producers loosely grouped films in generic categories. Genre movies allow for an economy of expression through conventions and iconography. Colin McArthur provides a vivid example of the shorthand of generic expressivity in his comparison of specific shots from two gangster films from different periods, *Little Caesar* (1931) and *The Harder They Fall* (1956). Both films offer an image of three men in doorways wearing 'large hats and heavy coats' and standing in triangular formation, the dominant character at the front and flanked by two underlings behind. As McArthur notes, the repetition of certain visual patterns in genre movies allows audiences to know 'immediately what to expect of them by their physical attributes, their dress and deportment. It knows, too, by the disposition of the figures, which is dominant, which subordinate' (1972: 23). This system of signification, developed over time and with repetition, served well the fast pace of classic narration in films intended to be shown as part of a double bill that changed frequently.

In the classic studio system, genre movies are like Ford's assembly line cars with interchangeable parts. The James Bond series continues because of the formula – lots of action, fancy gadgets, beautiful women and colourful villains – despite the changes in directors, writers and even the actors playing Bond himself. Individual genre films may lift elements from one genre and put them into another, as *The Band Wagon* (1953) incorporates film noir and the detective film into the climactic 'The Girl Hunt' ballet. In the western *Red River* (1948), a young and softly-spoken cowhand on the cattle drive gently admits that if the drive succeeds his goal is to buy new shoes for his wife; when he is the first casualty during a stampede, audiences recognise a convention borrowed from countless war movies. Recombinant genre movies like *Abbott and Costello Meet Frankenstein* (1948) and *Billy the Kid vs. Dracula* (1966) mix elements from seemingly disparate genres. More recently, movies like *Freddy vs. Jason* (2003) and *Alien vs. Predator* (2004), both of which are simultaneously recombinant movies and sequels, show the same process at work despite the end of the studio era.

By the 1930s the Hollywood studios had achieved vertical integration, controlling distribution and exhibition as well as production. In response, the federal government initiated anti-trust proceedings against the major studios (MGM, Paramount, RKO, Twentieth Century Fox and Warner Bros.), which culminated in 1948 with the US Supreme Court ruling in what has become known as 'the Paramount Decision' which decreed that the studios were engaging in monopolistic practices and had to divest their exhibition chains. The studios eventually diversified by concentrating on the new medium of television as well as on film production, and on establishing themselves as the major national exporter of films around the world, but the practice of block booking and the steady output of dependable B features soon ended. With the breakdown of the studio system came the end of the Production Code, the self-monitoring system of censorship established by the Motion Picture Association of America in 1930 as a response to growing criticism from conservative forces within American society, which was replaced by a ratings system in 1968.

Yet despite its constraints, the studio system did provide a stable context for filmmakers to work with consistency and to be expressive. As Robin Wood notes, Hollywood is one of the few historical instances of a true communal art, 'a great creative workshop, comparable to Elizabethan London or the Vienna of Mozart, where hundreds of talents have come together to evolve a common language' (1968: 9). The justly famous opening scene of Howard Hawks' *Rio Bravo* (1959) tells us almost everything we need to know about the heroes played by John Wayne and Dean Martin well before the first word of dialogue is spoken. Hawks uses the conventions of the western to express his sense of professionalism, heroism and self-respect, which would not have been possible without the established conventions of the genre as his raw material (Pye 2003: 213). As André Bazin observed long ago, 'the American cinema is a classical art, but why not then admire in it what is most admirable ... the genius of the system, the richness of its ever-vigorous tradition', which he praised apart from the achievement of individual films and directors (1968: 154).

Elements of Genre

Whether they are expensive epics or egregious exploitation, genre movies are composed of certain common elements. However we may define specific genres, the films that we choose to include in any generic category necessarily share certain of those elements. Yet generic description must always avoid slipping into evaluation by reifying generic patterns of a historical period as norms. 'Classic' should refer to a particular type of western but, confusingly, in common parlance it also denotes greatness, which is a judgement of value. Altman rightly observes that traditional film genre criticism has the unfortunate tendency to emphasise 'genre fixity', to think of genres as permanent (1999: 50). Both Bazin and Robert Warshow are guilty of this in writing about the 'classic' western, and although they may be forgiven because they lacked both a critical tradition and the historical vantage point we have today, many other critics have fallen into the same trap.

conventions

In any art form or medium, conventions are frequently-used stylistic techniques or narrative devices typical of (but not necessarily unique to) particular generic traditions. Bits of dialogue, musical figures or styles and patterns of *mise-en-scène* are all aspects of movies that, repeated from film to film within a genre, become established as conventions. In anarchic comedies like *Duck Soup* (1933), Groucho Marx addresses the camera directly, breaking down the cinematic equivalent of the proscenium or 'fourth wall'. Such moments are violations of convention analogous to those normative values lampooned in these films' narratives. Despite the obvious breach of realism in such a convention it is accepted by audiences within its generic context, contributing to the pleasure we derive from genre movies.

Conventions function as an implied agreement between makers and consumers to accept certain artificialities, but such artificialities work in specific contexts. In musicals the narrative halts for the production numbers wherein characters break into song and dance; often the characters perform for the camera (rather than for an audience within the film) and are accompanied by non-diegetic music that seems suddenly to materialise from nowhere. Like the direct address to the camera in comedy, this convention of the musical is fundamentally anti-realist. For this reason it is not as readily acceptable in the context of dramatic genre films, which typically invite spectators to suspend their disbelief and invest in the exciting illusions of reality they construct. Thus the opening of *West Side Story* (1961) seems momentarily jarring when Russ Tamblyn and his gang of Jets, apparently in a teen film about juvenile delinquency, begin to pirouette and dance on the concrete streets of New York City.

Conventions also include aspects of style associated with particular genres. For example, melodrama is characterised by an excessively stylised *mise-en-scène*, while film noir commonly employs low-key lighting and narrative flashbacks. Horror films often rely on tight framing, preparing for the inevitable hand that suddenly reaches into the frame for someone's shoulder. Even the graphic style of opening credits may be conventional, as in the case of the 'Wild West font' often found at the beginnings of westerns, evocative of the rough-hewn wood of pioneer homesteads, or the scrawled and edgily kinetic credit style of serial-killer films like *Se7en* (1995) that suggest a psychological disturbance haunting the killer.

Mainstream cinema also features numerous aural conventions on the soundtrack involving dialogue, music and sound effects. Film scoring in all genres often featuring Wagnerian leitmotifs associated with particular characters or places is commonly used to enhance a desired emotional effect in support of the story. This convention is parodied in Mel Brooks' *Blazing Saddles* (1974) when the black sheriff (Cleavon Little) rides through the desert accompanied by the incongruous tune 'April in Paris', and then passes by Count Basie and his Orchestra inexplicably present, playing one of their signature tunes in the wilderness. Different types of musical accompaniment are conventional in particular genres. Sweeping strings are common in romantic melodramas, while electronic music or the theremin is used in science fiction for its futuristic connotations.

The familiarity of conventions allows for parody, which becomes possible only when conventions are known to audiences. As discussed in Chapter 2, much of the humour of Mel Brooks' film parodies depends upon viewers being familiar with specific genre films. Conventions can also be used by filmmakers for disturbing purposes precisely because viewers expect them. George A. Romero's undermining of numerous conventions of the classic horror film in *Night of the Living Dead* (1968), also discussed later, is one of the main reasons the film had such a powerful effect on audiences when first released.

iconography
The term 'iconography' derives from art historian Erwin Panofsky's discussion of Renaissance art, wherein he suggested that themes or concepts were expressed by symbolically-charged objects and events. Genre critics such as Lawrence Alloway adapted the idea of iconography – that familiar

symbols in works of art have cultural meaning beyond the context of the individual work in which they appear – to the medium of cinema. Icons are second-order symbols, in that their symbolic meaning is not necessarily a connection established within the individual text, but is already symbolic because of their use across a number of similar previous texts. While Alloway's discussion of violent American crime films focuses more on story, theme and cinematic style than on objects within the *mise-en-scène*, Ed Buscombe (2003) concentrates on the iconography of the western in drawing a distinction between a film's inner and outer forms. For Buscombe, inner form refers to a film's themes, while outer form refers to the various objects that are to be found repeatedly in genre movies – in the western, for example, horses, wagons, buildings, clothes and weapons.

In genre films, iconography refers to particular objects, archetypal characters and even specific actors. In the western, the cowboy who dresses all in black and wears two guns, holster tied to either thigh, is invariably a villainous gunfighter. This is the iconographic wardrobe of a generic type, bearing little relation to historical reality. Just as religious icons are always already infused with symbolic meaning, so is the iconography of genre films. In a horror film, when the hero wards off the vampire with a crucifix, religious iconography works in support of film iconography: symbolically, such scenes suggests that the traditional values embodied in Christianity (and, by extension, Western culture generally) are stronger than and will defeat whatever threatening values are assigned to the monster in any given vampire film.

Iconography may also refer to the general *mise-en-scène* of a genre, as in the case of low-key lighting and Gothic design in the horror film or the visual excess of the melodrama. Gunbelts, Stetson hats and spurs are icons of the western, just as chiaroscuro lighting is iconographic of film noir. Like conventions, iconography provides genres with a visual shorthand for conveying information and meaning succinctly. Pinstripe suits, dark shirts and white ties define which side of the law characters are on in the gangster film as typically as black hats and white hats differentiate hero and villain in the western.

Of course, while the icons of genre films may have culturally determined meanings, the interpretation or value attached to them is hardly fixed. Rather, the particulars of their representation in each genre film mark the relation of outer form to inner form, and are indicators of the film's attitude and theme. Although a crucifix in a horror film is an icon of Christianity and dominant ideology, the film itself may either critique or endorse that ideology. In the western, the town always represents civil-isation, but every film will have a different view of it. The town in, say, *The Gunfighter* (1950) has children and domestic spaces, representing the familial stability that Gregory Peck's ageing gunman can only long for, while in *McCabe and Mrs. Miller* (1971) the town springs up around a muddy, makeshift brothel, suggesting that base desire is at the core of civilisation. Even more pointedly, Sam Peckinpah put a gallows in the centre of town in *Pat Garrett and Billy the Kid* (1973), indicating the propensity towards violence at the heart of civilisation.

Buscombe clearly shows how Peckinpah criticises modern society through the careful manipulation of the iconography of the town in the opening scene of *Ride the High Country* (aka *Guns in the Afternoon*, 1962). As the film begins, a visibly ageing Joel McCrea (star of over a dozen earlier westerns, including the 1946 version of *The Virginian*), rides into town during a Fourth of July celebration. American civilisation has advanced on the frontier, as signified by the brick buildings rather than the convent-ional clapboard structures of the typical western movie town. A uniformed policeman instead of the singular sheriff with a badge suggests institut-ionalised law, while the lampposts and automobiles tell us that historically the period of the Wild West is over. People are cheering and McCrea thinks the cheers are for him, but in fact they are cheering for riders in a race between horses and a camel. As Buscombe notes, 'a horse in a western is not just an animal, but a symbol of dignity, grace and power. These qualit-ies are mocked by having it compete with a camel; and to add insult to injury, the camel wins' (2003: 23).

The deflating treatment of the horse as icon is emblematic of this film's general subversion of the genre's typically positive view of civilisation. The town may be commemorating the birth of the nation, but Peckinpah ques-tions the gospel of progress that is so visibly evident there. The celebration of the nation's founding is depicted in the film as a carnival, a decadent display complete with exotic dancing girls, hardly the expression of social and spiritual bonding that such celebrations are in John Ford's westerns. McCrea is almost run over by a car – a 'horseless carriage' – as he begins to cross the street, while the policeman, calling him an old-timer, shouts at him that he is in the way. The western hero is an anachronism as the film starts (later we see in a close-up that his shirt cuffs are frayed). Civilisation in *Ride the High Country* boasts technological progress, but Peckinpah ironically depicts it as morally retrograde. He shows the carnival from a high angle, as if judging from above, looking down in disapproval from a higher moral ground – the high country of the title.

setting
The physical space and time – where and when a film's story takes place – is more a defining quality of some genres than others. Musicals, for instance, can take place anywhere, from the actual streets and docks of New York City in *West Side Story* and *On the Town* (1949) to the supernatural village in *Brigadoon* (1954). Romantic comedies and dramas, like some science fiction, may span different eras, as in *Somewhere in Time* (1980) and *Kate and Leopold* (2001). In the gangster film the city weighs down on the protagonist – 'not the real city', as Warshow observes, 'but that dangerous and sad city of the imagination which is so much more important, which is the modern world' (1971a: 131). Warshow claims that gangsters dwell exclusively in the city, yet while most gangster films do take place in urban settings, important gangster movies like *The Petrified Forest* (1936), *High Sierra* (1941) and *Key Largo* (1948) do not.

When science fiction movies located in the future use contemporary architecture for settings rather than construct sets in the studio or with computer imaging, they suggest a more disturbing continuity between the present and the future, as in *THX 1138* (1971) which uses the San Francisco subway system, and the actual mall setting of *Logan's Run* (1976). Similarly, horror movies often use isolated and rural settings, and old dark houses with mysterious basements for psychological effect; but films such as *Rosemary's Baby* (1968) and *Dark Water* (2005) work by violating convention and setting stories in contemporary and familiar locales rather than in exoticised foreign spaces like Transylvania or Haiti.

By contrast, the western by definition is temporally restricted to the period of the Wild West (approximately 1865–1890) and geographically to the American frontier (broadly, between the Mississippi River and the west coast). Movies that change this setting to the present, such as *Lonely are the Brave* (1962) and *Hud* (1963), or 'easterns' like *Drums Along the Mohawk* (1939) and *The Last of the Mohicans* (1936, 1992), are considered exceptions to the norm, westerns for some viewers but not for others.

Yet movies such as *Coogan's Bluff* (1968) and *Crocodile Dundee II* (1988) that import elements of the western into the contemporary urban east are generally not thought of as westerns.

The relative fixity of the western setting allows the landscape in the genre to assume thematic weight. It may function as an objective correlative to the spiritual state of individual characters, as in Anthony Mann's westerns, or of society more generally, as in Ford's repeated use of Monument Valley. Don Siegel's *Two Mules for Sister Sarah* (1970) begins with a montage cutting between a cowboy (Clint Eastwood) riding through the wilderness and various animals in the environment: an owl, a rattlesnake, a cougar and a tarantula, the last of which is squashed by Eastwood's horse as he rides by. The animals are predatory which suggests the film's harsh view of life on the frontier, borne out in the plot which begins with three men preying sexually upon a woman and involves a French colonial army oppressing the Mexican people.

Ford's *My Darling Clementine* (1946) contains a famous scene in which Wyatt Earp (Henry Fonda) and Clementine Carter (Cathy Downs) join a dedication celebration for the partially-built church with the people of Tombstone. The scene deftly uses generic iconography to depict what John Cawelti calls 'the epic moment' of American history – that pivotal moment when civilisation comes to the wilderness (1985: 39). As Douglas Pye notes, Earp and Clementine walk down the main street of Tombstone, their linked arms roughly centred in the frame, as if down the aisle at a wedding, church bells solemnly tolling. Behind Earp lies the wilderness of Monument Valley, while behind Clementine are the town's buildings, representing community, commerce, civilisation (2003: 210–13). Their coupling here suggests the integration of the individualist western hero into the community. Christianity and nationalism provide the literal foundation of Ford's mythic American society, as the church floor is flanked by twin American flags on one side and the church steeple on the other. With these values, the film suggests, the church can be completed and the nation soundly built.

stories and themes
Most genre films, as instances of classic narrative cinema, are structured according to the principles outlined by David Bordwell in his discussion of standard Hollywood practice (Bordwell, Staiger & Thompson 1985). They feature a common dramatic construction, focusing on an individual hero

who must overcome obstacles to achieve a goal. A problem is introduced that creates a disturbance or 'disequilibrium' in the world of the story, and that must be resolved by the story's end. According to Bordwell, this primary dramatic arc of the classic narrative film, with its rise and fall action, is entwined with a secondary one that focuses on a heterosexual romance. Such stories also contain narrative closure, in which all plot strands are brought to resolution. For example, in many science fiction movies of the 1950s, such as *Gog* (1954) or *The Creature from the Black Lagoon* (1954), the hero combines masculine prowess with technology to defeat the monster, after which he wins the scientist's lovely assistant or daughter, along with the paternal blessing of the elderly scientist.

Genre movies take such social debates and tensions and cast them into formulaic narratives, condensing them into dramatic conflicts between individual characters and society or heroes and villains. Thomas Schatz observes that 'all film genres treat some form of threat – violent or otherwise – to the social order' (1981: 26). The gangster, the monster, the heroine of screwball comedy all threaten normative society in different ways. Some genre theorists argue that the overriding theme of genre films is some version of the individual in conflict with society, and that this tension represents the ongoing negotiation we all make between desire and restraint (what Freud called 'civilisation and its discontents'). This struggle is ongoing, hence the reason for both the popularity and the repetitiveness of genre films. Schatz distinguishes between what he calls genres of 'determinate' and 'indeterminate' space: the former involve a physical conflict in a convent-ionalised arena of conflict (main street at high noon in the western, the city's mean streets in the gangster film) and address social integration, with the physical threat to society forcefully eradicated; while the latter (the musical, melodrama, romantic comedy) are concerned more with social order, coding the conflict within the tribulations of a heterosexual relationship.

The extent to which a genre film achieves narrative closure is an important factor in reading its political implications. Closure – usually in the form of an upbeat or happy ending – is, like all conventions, artificial, since life, unlike such stories, continues. For this reason a lack of closure, suggesting that the lives of the characters carry on after the film ends, is associated more with realist films like *La Grande Illusion* (1937) and *Ladri di biciclette* (*Bicycle Thieves*, 1947) than with genre movies. Because films with closure leave the viewer with no unanswered questions about the fate of the major characters or the consequences of their actions, they are viewed as providing tidy but unrealistic solutions to real problems. Yet while closure may be provided by a film, it can be ironic, thus undercutting its own pretense at resolution. This may be the case in *Psycho* (1960), where the psychiatrist's concluding explanation of Norman Bates' mental illness reduces him to a mere 'case' but cannot possibly contain the universal dark impulses the film has succeeded in encouraging in the audience (Wood 1989: 149–50).

In the wake of European art cinema definitive closure has become less common in Hollywood film today than in the past, but the reasons for this are as much historical as aesthetic. In the horror films of the studio era monsters were almost always defeated in the end, providing reassuring and confident messages to the audience, just as in the westerns of the period the cavalry came to the rescue when necessary. True, the occasional movie like *The Blob* (1958) leaves its ending tantalisingly ambiguous, since the gelatinous creature, seemingly invincible, is frozen and dropped in the Arctic; but this ending seemed motivated more by the possibility of a sequel than a social critique. By the late 1960s, however, with the mounting horrors of the Vietnam War and domestic violence escalating, many horror films tended to be open-ended, as in *Night of the Living Dead*, *Rosemary's Baby* and *It's Alive* (1974). Popular cinema at the time avoided addressing Vietnam directly and instead expressed the anxiety of an uncertain victory and increasing divisiveness on the home front coded within the context of genres.

characters, actors and stars
Discussing characters in literature, novelist E. M. Forster distinguished two kinds of fictional characters: flat and round. Flat characters, which also may be 'types' or 'caricatures', are built around one idea or quality; it is only as other attributes (that is, 'depth') are added that characters begin 'to curve toward the round' (1927: 67). In genre movies characters are more often recognisable types rather than psychologically complex characters, like black hats and white hats in the western, although they can be rounded as well. The femme fatale is a conventional character in film noir, like the comic sidekick, schoolmarm and gunfighter in the western. Ethnic characters are often flat stereotypes in genre movies: the Italian mobster, the

black drug dealer, the Arab terrorist, the cross-section of soldiers in the war film's platoon. While flat characters are usually considered a failure in works that aspire to originality, in genre works they are not necessarily a flaw because of their shorthand efficiency.

In genre movies, character types often provide similar kinds of actions and purposes within the story. Structuralist critic Vladimir Propp refers to these repeating appearances in generic narratives as 'functions', which he defines as the acts of characters in relation to their 'significance for the course of the action' (1968: 21). So, for example, both Yoda in the *Star Wars* films and Kesuke Miyagi (Pat Morita) in *The Karate Kid* (1984) are 'donors' who provide the hero with both a test and help in his quest. Another way of thinking about characters in the context of genre is offered by Northrop Frye's concept of modes. As Frye identifies them, there are five modes of fictional narration: from myth (the hero is superior to other men and his environment, a super-hero or god), romance (the hero is superior in degree, marvellous but mortal, like Hawkeye or Batman), high mimetic (the hero is superior in degree to other men but not to his environment, as with all tragic heroes), low mimetic (the hero is superior neither to other men nor to the natural world, but is one of us) and ironic (the protagonist is an anti-hero, inferior to ourselves in terms of power or intelligence). In *Raiders of the Lost Ark* (1981) Indiana Jones (Harrison Ford) is a romantic hero because he succeeds in his quest against all odds (although at times he verges on mythic status, as when he manages to hang onto a submerged German submarine crossing the Atlantic Ocean); by contrast, the unfortunate protagonist of *Detour* (1945) is an ironic anti-hero who, trapped by circumstances beyond his control, finds himself a doomed murderer.

Of course, characters are embodied by actors, all of whom have distinct physical characteristics. The hard-boiled detective Philip Marlowe is different as played by Dick Powell (*Murder, My Sweet*, 1944), Humphrey Bogart (*The Big Sleep*, 1946) or Elliott Gould (*The Long Goodbye*, 1973). Some actors (for example, Paul Muni and Johnny Depp) are known for chameleon-like performances, but many, whether they are featured stars or supporting actors, often play variations of a type. For this reason, they are often cast in similar films within the same genre and become associated with it. Fred Astaire is always thought of in relation to the musical, Cary Grant with screwball comedy and, of course, John Wayne with the western, even though all these actors also appeared in other kinds of films. Clint Eastwood's strong association with the western lends added depth to such non-western roles as the tough detective Harry Callahan in *Dirty Harry* (1971) and its sequels.

Character actors contribute to the look of particular genres, populating the worlds of genre movies and becoming part of their iconography. Often they are known to viewers as vaguely familiar faces rather than by name. Richard Jaeckel, Jack Elam, Chill Wills, Paul Fix and Slim Pickens all appeared in countless westerns, so when they are in the same cast and many of them die in *Pat Garrett and Billy the Kid*, the film may be read as being as much about the death of the genre as it is a story about particular characters. Soviet filmmaker Sergei Eisenstein, following from the theatrical tradition of *commedia dell'arte* where actors perform types rather than individual characters, developed an approach to casting which he called typage. Eisenstein cast actors according to physical qualities that provided the audience with visual cues about them: so, for example, in his films capitalists are always overweight fat cats, a sign of their material acquisitiveness and greed. The iconographic casting in mainstream genre movies is not unlike typage, for actors are often cast in variations of roles because of their physical attributes. Arnold Schwarzenegger's body determined that he would star in action films; the incongruity of the muscular actor appearing in a different generic context provides the comic premises for *Kindergarten Cop* (1990) and *Junior* (1994).

Stars embody in concrete, physical form society's values at particular historical moments. Raymond Durgnat writes that 'the stars are a reflection in which the public studies and adjusts its own image of itself ... The social history of a nation can be written in terms of its film stars' (1967: 137–8). Of course, the same might be said about the genre movies in which stars appear. Indeed, stars and genres reinforce each other.

Actors sometimes offer definitive performances that forever associate them with a particular role, as we might associate Anthony Perkins with Norman Bates, no matter in which films he subsequently appeared. Sometimes these roles assume iconographic proportion, as in the case of Bela Lugosi's portrayal of Dracula. Actors who succeed at playing a certain generic type are often trapped by such roles, fated to be typecast as similar characters. Dick Powell began as a romantic ('juvenile') lead in several Warner Bros. musicals in the early 1930s, but managed to reshape his image entirely in the following decade, playing a tough guy in such film noirs as *Murder, My Sweet, Cornered* (1945) and *Pitfall* (1948).

Some actors become icons because of their performances in genre films, their faces and bodies instantly recognisable in the culture. John Wayne had such a strong iconographic presence as the rugged American individualist and western hero that the death of his character, Will Anderson, at the hands of villainous Bruce Dern in *The Cowboys* (1972) is as shockingly unexpected as Marion Crane's death in *Psycho*. Also, since Anderson is killed in full view of the group of adolescent boys in his charge without sacrificing his dignity, his death becomes a statement about the death of the classic western hero. This theme is even more explicit in Wayne's last film, *The Shootist* (1976), in which he plays a gunfighter who is dying of cancer, as was Wayne himself at the time.

Because actors may become typecast, they can be cast in genre movies against type, as in the case of William Holden playing the leader of *The Wild Bunch* (1969) or Tom Cruise as a hit man in *Collateral* (2004). In the famous opening of Sergio Leone's *Once Upon a Time in the West* (1968), a Mexican family enjoying a pleasant picnic meal in front of their hacienda is suddenly and brutally gunned down by unseen assailants. In a long take, the killers ride in from the distance and eventually we are able to discern that the leader is a grim-faced, blue-eyed Henry Fonda – the same softly-spoken man who was Abraham Lincoln in *Young Mr. Lincoln* (1939) and Tom Joad in *The Grapes of Wrath* (1940). The moment has a greater emotional impact than it would if the actor had been a familiar Hollywood heavy.

viewers and audiences

Genres are dependent upon audiences for both their existence and meaning. Well before the first scholarly writing on film genre, the idea of genre circulated in public thinking. Almost from the beginning movies have been promoted in the media primarily through their generic affiliations. They signal to prospective viewers the type of story as well as the kind of pleasure they are likely to offer and assist them in choosing which movies to see. For example, some viewers dislike horror films because they do not enjoy being frightened or because they disapprove of violence. Some people prefer different genres at different times, wanting to watch a comedy, say, if they have had a bad day. Fans of particular genres comprise what Rick Altman calls 'constellated communities' of readers (1999: 161 ff.).

Fans of horror films, for example, form a distinct subculture, with their own fanzines, memorabilia, websites and discussion lists.

Genre films work by engaging viewers through an implicit contract. They encourage certain expectations on the part of spectators, which are in turn based on viewer familiarity with the conventions. As Robert Warshow observes, the familiarity of viewers with generic convention creates 'its own field of reference' (1971a: 130). Spectators appreciate the climactic fight in *Terror in a Texas Town* (1958) in which the hero, a former whaler, meets the villainous gunfighter at high noon in the centre of town with his harpoon instead of a pistol, only because of the westerns they have seen. Familiarity with a generic field of reference allows spectators to enjoy variations, however slight, in a given film. Warshow also writes that for viewers of genre films 'originality is to be welcomed only in the degree that it intensifies the expected experience without fundamentally altering it' (ibid.), although this claim does not adequately explain the popularity of revisionist or 'anti-genre' films. The act of reading genre films implies active readers who bring their generic knowledge to bear in watching movies. A postmodern horror pastiche like *Scream* (1996) depends upon its viewers being generically literate.

The opening of Peckinpah's *Bring Me the Head of Alfredo Garcia* (1974) offers an instructive example of how spectator knowledge can be mobilised by a genre film to generate complex meaning. Set in Mexico, the film begins with an idyllic scene of a young woman sitting peacefully by a tranquil pond with swans. But the scene is abruptly interrupted as the girl is informed that her father wants to see her, and she is escorted to him. Surrounded by armed men and watching women, the girl's stern, authoritarian father demands to know who has made her pregnant. When she refuses to answer he orders one of his men to break her hand, after which she reveals the man's identity to be Alfredo Garcia. The father then makes the demand for revenge that serves as the film's title. Until this point Peckinpah has carefully inserted numerous icons of the western (boots, horses, guns, spurs) and included nothing that is clearly contemporary. We are prompted to read the film as a western – a reading also encouraged by knowledge of Peckinpah's previous films, almost all of which were westerns. Then, immediately upon the father's enraged demand, Peckinpah cuts to shots of cars and motorcycles roaring out of the ranch and a jet screaming on a runway, after which it is clear that the story has a contemporary setting.

Because of its western elements, the film has led us to think about how cruelly patriarchal the world was in the past; then we are caught up short with the sudden, grating intrusiveness of technology, revealing that the story is in fact a contemporary one and that, according to the film, such abuse is equally true today.

Problems of Definition

Fundamental to defining any genre is the question of corpus, of what films in fact constitute its history. Janet Staiger suggests that there are four ways to approach genre definition, each with its own limitations. The *idealist method*, which judges films against a predetermined standard, is proscriptive in that certain films are privileged over others to the extent that they remain close to the chosen model; the *empiricist method* involves circular logic in that the films selected already have been chosen as representing the genre; the *a priori method*, in which common generic elements are selected in advance; and the *social convention method*, which is problematic in how cultural consensus is determined (2003: 186–7).

The empiricist method is perhaps the most common. Andrew Tudor explains a major problem of genre definition, which he terms 'the empiricist dilemma':

> To take a genre such as a 'western', analyse it, and list its principle characteristics, is to beg the question that we must first isolate the body of films that are westerns. But they can only be isolated on the basis of the 'principle characteristics' which can only be discovered *from the films themselves* after they have been isolated. (1973: 135)

Tudor's solution to this problem of definition is to rely on what he calls a 'common cultural consensus', that is, to analyse works that almost everyone would agree belong to a particular genre, and generalise out from there. This method is acceptable, he concludes, because 'genre is what we collectively believe it to be' (1973: 139). Tudor's solution offers a pragmatically useful approach that has been taken up by many genre critics.

Nevertheless, a problem with the various genres that have been established by common cultural consensus, as several scholars have noted, is that different genres are designated according to different criteria. Such genres as the crime film, science fiction and the western are defined by setting and narrative content. However, horror, pornography and comedy are defined or conceived around the intended emotional effect of the film upon the viewer. Linda Williams (2003) has referred to horror, melodrama and porn as 'body genres' because of the strong physical response – fear, tears and sexual arousal, respectively – elicited by each. The extent to which films of these genres produce the intended response in viewers is commonly used as a determining factor in judging how good they are.

But however defined, generic categories must be useful. Categories such as narrative, documentary and abstract or experimental, while they do cover the range of possible types of filmmaking, are too broad to be very useful for genre criticism. Both Stuart Kaminsky (1974: 9) and Tom Leitch (2002: 1–18) acknowledge the difficulty of defining the genre of crime films, since it includes gangster films, detective and mystery films, action films, police films and heist movies. Kaminsky, however, goes on to discuss comedy as a genre, even though the category might be said to include such different forms as the screwball comedy, romantic comedy, slapstick, black comedy and parody.

Jim Collins has argued that since the 1980s Hollywood movies have been characterised by an 'ironic hybridisation' that seeks to combine elements from previously pure or discrete genres. As examples, Collins cites *Back to the Future III* (1990), a western and science fiction film, as well as *Blade Runner* (1982), *Blue Velvet* (1986) and *Who Framed Roger Rabbit* (1988) (1993: 245). However, Janet Staiger has convincingly countered the notion of genre purity, arguing that 'Hollywood films have never been "pure" – that is, easily arranged into categories. All that has been pure has been sincere attempts to find order among variety' (2003: 185). She cites *Abbott and Costello Meet Frankenstein* (1948), a film emblematic of Hollywood studio practice in that Universal Studios was recycling the conventions of its earlier genre films to fit with its new stars (2003: 192). Staiger, as in her earlier work with Bordwell and Thompson (1985: 16–17), concludes that nearly all Hollywood films were hybrids insofar as they tended to combine one type of generic plot – a romance – with others, a point with which Steve Neale heartily concurs (2003: 172).

Clearly genre movies have always been hybrid, combinative in practice. *Stagecoach* (1939), one of the most famous and important westerns ever made, was described as a '*Grand Hotel* on wheels' on its release, and it also contains elements of the road movie and disaster film as well. Vivian Sobchack notes that the monster movie sits uneasily between the horror film and science fiction (1980: 47). Movies such as *The Thing* (1951), *It! The Terror from Beyond Space* (1958) and the film on which it was in part based, *Alien* (1979), all combine elements of science fiction and horror, visually turning spaceships and laboratories into the equivalent of haunted houses.

Case Study: The Strange Case of Film Noir

Film noir (literally, 'black film') is a generic category developed initially by critics rather than the industry. It was French critics who first used the term to describe a number of dark and stylised Hollywood movies that began to appear after World War Two and into the 1950s. These movies featured corrupt characters in the ruthless, fatalistic world. Many film noirs were B movies, which ironically added to rather than detracted from their expressiveness, as their frequent lack of high production values tended to emphasise the seemliness of their fictional worlds. Their downbeat vision and expressionist stylisation constituted a remarkable divergence from the traditional optimism and plentitude of Hollywood.

The visual conventions of film noir include such expressionist elements of *mise-en-scène* as chiaroscuro lighting, contrasts of dark and light in the image, imbalanced compositions that suggest powerlessness and geometric compositions that imply entrapment and doom. Most noirs are set in the city, its impersonal and alienating qualities reflecting the decadent and cynical world they depict. In noirs such as *The Naked City* (1948), the city is a palpable presence, taking on a menacing quality that threatens to overwhelm the individuals who dwell in it. The opening shot of *Force of Evil* (1948) shows a church dwarfed and crowded by skyscrapers – an image that, in sharp contrast to the church scene in *My Darling Clementine*, bespeaks the secular motivations of greed and desire that have squeezed out spiritual or religious values in the world of noir. Film noir's iconography includes puddles, rainwater, mirrors, windows and blinking neon lights, all reflecting the darkness of the souls within the asphalt jungle. As Paul Schrader notes, the location photography of many noirs would seem antithetical to the stylisation of noir, but 'the best noir technicians simply made

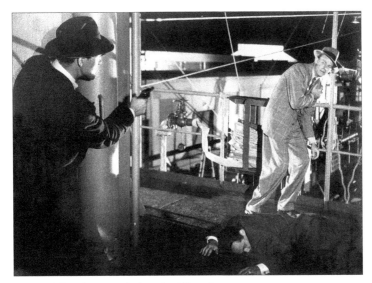

Figure 1 *T-Men:* the expressionist style of film noir

all the world a sound stage, directing unnatural and expressionistic lighting onto realistic settings' (2003: 233).

Plots in film noir frequently involve some variation of a man lured into a criminal act, often murder, by an attractive but dangerous woman, ultimately leading to mutual self-destruction (Damico 1978: 54). Narrative construction is frequently complex, as in *The Big Sleep*, which features multiple storylines and murders. The interweaving of characters and their motives is so layered that the film's director, Howard Hawks, confessed he was unable to figure out the perpetrator of one of them. Often told in voice-over with flashbacks, noir narratives suggest a fatalistic, entrapping world in which action has already been determined, as in *Out of the Past* (1947). Protagonists are often caught in a web of circumstances beyond their control, as exemplified by the unfortunate drifter who inadvertently commits murder in *Detour*. In *Sunset Boulevard* (1950) the protagonist narrator is already dead when the story begins, telling his story from beyond the grave, and the poor salesman in *D.O.A.* (1950), after being fatally poisoned with a radioactive isotope, seeks to capture his own killer before expiring in the final scene.

Noir protagonists are almost exclusively male, and many critics have suggested that they reflected the disturbances to traditional notions of masculinity and gender roles caused by the war and post-war readjustment. The period was particularly fraught in this regard, as popular culture sought to reposition the proper place of women in the domestic sphere, which they had been encouraged to abandon, to join the home front work force; this new empowerment for women is expressed in the stark dichotomy of noir's representation of women as either domestic and bland or as sexualised femmes fatales. Frank Krutnik (1991), for example, argues that film noir expresses a crisis in masculinity that reveals male anxiety about loss of power in a post-war society, while feminist critics see some women in film noir as smart, independent, active characters who inevitably are punished within the films' narratives for their independence.

Noir is commonly explained as the result of several converging influences, most significant being the influx to Hollywood preceding and during the Nazi rise to power in the early 1930s of many directors, actors, cinematographers and others involved in German expressionist cinema. Also, there was a renewed interest in realism during and after World War Two, inspired by war reportage and Italian neo-realism. This influence is apparent in the location photography in such noirs as *House on 92nd Street* (1945), *Kiss of Death* (1947) and *The Naked City*. The American or 'hard-boiled' style of detective fiction by such writers as Dashiell Hammett, Raymond Chandler and James M. Cain provided many of the stories adapted by noir. It has been said as well that film noir also depicted a sense of post-war disillusionment that was in part a delayed reaction to the enforced optimism of popular culture during the Depression and the war years, as seen in the noir films about returning veterans discovering unfaithful wives or suffering from war trauma, such as *Cornered*, *The Blue Dahlia* (1946) and *Ride the Pink Horse* (1947) (Schrader 2003).

David Bordwell argues that noir was not a genre because the term did not exist in popular discourse: 'Producers and consumers both recognise a genre as a distinct entity; nobody set out to make or see a film noir in the sense that people deliberately chose to make a western, a comedy or a musical' (Bordwell, Staiger & Thompson 1985: 74). Not alone, Bordwell sees noir as a style, not a genre. Like the broad category of comedy, the noir style seeps into any genre, including westerns (*Pursued*, 1947; *Rancho Notorious*, 1952) and even comedy – most famously, when George Bailey

Figure 2 *Pursued*: noir style in the western

(James Stewart) imagines what the town of Bedford Falls would be like if he had never been born in Frank Capra's *It's a Wonderful Life* (1946). The expressionist conventions of the noir style can be found in several other genres, including caper films, detective films, gangster films and thrillers.

Another argument against defining film noir as a genre is that it had a specific time span, conventionally seen as extending from John Huston's *The Maltese Falcon* in 1941 to Orson Welles' *Touch of Evil* in 1958. Certainly by the late 1950s, the evolving production values of Hollywood cinema undermined the noir style and the look of Hollywood movies changed. Techniques such as widescreen and colour, introduced to combat a dwindling audience because of the growing popularity of television, provided a look that was antithetical to that of noir: the vivid intensity of colour processes such as Technicolor countered noir's black-and-white chiaroscuro lighting, while widescreen images opened up its entrapping *mise-en-scène*. Further, a contributing industrial factor was that B films were no longer guaranteed distribution as the bottom half of a double feature, but were now threatened by Hollywood's move toward the single-feature epic or blockbuster.

But in 1974 the commercial and critical success of Roman Polanski's *Chinatown* – a paranoid thriller about a utilities conspiracy set in 1930s Los Angeles, the city and time associated with the classic 'hard-boiled' detective novel – brought about a renewed interest in film noir and spurred the production of a cycle of neo-noirs beginning with the British versions of *Farewell, My Lovely* (1975, a remake of *Murder, My Sweet*) and *The Big Sleep* (1978, original 1946), both starring noir icon Robert Mitchum as Chandler's private detective Philip Marlowe, and *Body Heat* (1981), with a steamy but doomed romance indebted to *The Postman Always Rings Twice* (1946). Later, the remakes of *D.O.A.* (1988) and *The Big Clock* (1948, remade as *No Way Out*, 1987), as well as the science fiction noirs (techno-noir) *Blade Runner* and *Dark City* (1998), in which a noirish world is constructed on an asteroid for unaware humans as an alien experiment, show that noir remains a vibrant generic tradition. Some directors such as Joel and Ethan Coen (*Blood Simple*, 1984; *Fargo*, 1996; *The Man Who Wasn't There*, 2001) and John Dahl (*Red Rock West*, 1992; *The Last Seduction*, 1994) are associated with neo-noir. Furthermore, the 1990s cycle of erotic thrillers, beginning with the box office success of *Fatal Attraction* (1987), employs elements of noir in the tradition of *The Postman Always Rings Twice* (remade in 1981). The return of film noir after more than a decade suggests that it was not temporally bound, and some critics have made a convincing case for noir as a genre with distinct narrative and visual conventions.

2   GENRE AND SOCIETY

Ritual and Myth

Traditionally, the term 'myth' refers to a society's shared stories, usually involving gods and mythic heroes, that explain the nature of the universe and the relation of the individual to it. Such mythic narratives embody and express a society's rituals, institutions and values. In Western culture, myths, initially transmitted orally and then in print, have been disseminated by mass culture since the late nineteenth century. In the twentieth century, genre films, with their repetitions and variations of a few basic plots, are prime instances of mass-mediated contemporary myth. As Thomas Sobchack writes,

> The Greeks knew the stories of the gods and the Trojan War in the same way we know about hoodlums and gangsters and G-men and the taming of the frontier and the never-ceasing struggle of the light of reason and the cross with the powers of darkness, not through first-hand experience but through the media. (2003: 103)

In mass-mediated society, we huddle around movie screens instead of campfires for our mythic tales. Comparable to myths, genre movies may be understood as secular stories that seek to address and sometimes seemingly resolve our problems and dilemmas, some specifically historical and others more deeply rooted in our collective psyches. The ritualistic aspects of movie-going are perhaps most apparent in the phenomenon of group spectator interaction with cult movies, as in the case of the Waverly Cinema screenings of *The Rocky Horror Picture Show* (1975) where audiences responded to certain lines of dialogue with predetermined comments and actions. But this phenomenon operates in a less dramatic fashion with all genre movies, since they trigger viewers' expectations and engage reading strategies that are dependent on the framework of genre. This is true in the experience of any genre film, whether it fulfils, violates or subverts generic convention. In their mythic capacity, genre films provide a means for cultural dialogue, engaging their audiences in a shared discourse that reaffirms, challenges and tests cultural values and identity.

Shane (1953) is often cited as a deliberately mythic representation of the western hero. As the film opens, Shane (Alan Ladd) rides into town from the mountain wilderness, descending into the realm of mortals like a buckskinned, luminous god. Shane has greater speed with a gun than anyone else – 'superior in kind' to other men, as Frye puts it (1970: 33). To emphasise Shane's mythic proportion, the story is told from the perspective of young Joey (Brandon de Wilde); along with him we look up to Shane from a low angle (which also serves the practical function of masking Ladd's short stature), monumentalising him. When Shane rides off at the end, heading once again into the wilderness like so many western heroes before him, he ascends into the mountains as if into heaven, ultimately riding out of the frame as if to some unearthly realm beyond the world of mortals. In the post-war era of escalating Cold War tensions and the rise of the military-industrial complex, *Shane* offered a reassuring myth of a western (American) hero who will mete swift justice on behalf of the small farmer and average citizen. As if a god apart from mortal affairs, Shane has temporarily joined the human world in order to restore equilibrium to the social order, a clear instance of the mythic dimension of genre films.

As *Shane* shows, while genre films function as ritual and myth, they are also inevitably about the time they are made, not when they are set. Science fiction works by extrapolating aspects of contemporary society into a hypothetical future, parallel or alien society; thus the genre always imposes today on tomorrow, the here onto there. Yet even such genres as the western and gangster film, although ostensibly focused on particular periods of American history, do the same. The heroes of genre stories embody values a culture holds virtuous; villains embody evil in specific ways. As discussed in separate case studies later on, *Stagecoach* is as

Figure 3 *Shane*: the camera and Joey look up to Shane

much about late 1930s and New Deal America as *Little Big Man* (1970) is steeped in the Vietnam era.

Structural anthropologist Claude Lévi-Strauss (1977) claimed that all cultural myths are structured according to binary pairs of opposite terms. This approach is inviting for the analysis of genre films, which tend to work by reducing complex conflicts to the equivalent of black hats versus white

31

hats. In his influential study of the western, Jim Kitses (1970) first maps out a series of clear binary oppositions that are all variations of the conflict between wilderness and civilisation, then proceeds to analyse the work of several directors associated with the genre. Kitses' work has influenced virtually all subsequent studies of the western, yet critics have not mapped out in any comparable detail the binary structures of other genres with the possible exception of the horror film.

History and Ideology

Entertainment inevitably contains, reflects and promulgates ideology. It is in this sense of entertainment as ideology that Roland Barthes uses the term *myth*. Showing how mythic connotations are conveyed in a wide variety of cultural artefacts and events from mundane consumer products to sporting events like wrestling, Barthes argues that 'the very principle of myth [is that] it transforms history into nature' (1972: 129) – that is, cultural myths endorse the dominant values of the society that produces them as right and natural, while marginalising and delegitimising alternatives and others. With the rise of semiology in the 1970s and into the 1980s, critical interest shifted from the signified of films to the practices of signification – that is, from what a film 'means' to how it produces meaning. Barthes' attempt to deconstruct the mythic codes of cultural texts appealed both to scholars wishing to demonstrate that genres were little more than bourgeois illusionism, conservative propaganda for passive spectators, and those who saw the codes of genre as providing the possibility for ideological contestation and empowerment. Melodrama and horror proved to be particularly fruitful genres for such analyses, while more recent theoretical work on representation has opened up space for the analysis of genre and sexuality, race, class and national identity.

Although Barthes addressed cinema hardly at all, his ideas about cultural myth have influenced much subsequent work on film. His description of cultural myth applies perfectly to genre movies: 'Myth does not deny things, on the contrary, its function is to talk about them; simply, it purifies them, it makes them innocent, it gives them a clarity which is not that of an explanation but that of a statement of fact' (1972: 143). The elements of cultural myth that Barthes identifies can all be found in genre films: the stripping of history from the narrative, the tendency toward proverbs and the inability to imagine the Other. Classic narrative cinema, like myth, makes culture into nature: the movies are told in ways that eliminate the markers of their narration, as if they were a window onto the world and its truths rather than a constructed frame that is a representation. Genre movies also speak in proverbs through conventions: the romantic couple come together to marry and live happily ever after, crime does not pay, there are things in the universe that man was not meant to know. In genre movies, as Barthes says of cultural myth generally, the Other becomes monstrous, as in horror films, or exoticised, as in adventure films. In westerns, Indians are either demonised as savage heathens or romanticised as noble savages, but rarely treated as rounded characters with their own culture.

From this perspective, genre movies tend to be read as ritualised endorsements of dominant ideology. So the western is not really about a specific period in American history, but mantra of Manifest Destiny and the 'winning' of the west. The genre thus offers a series of mythic endorsements of American individualism, colonialism and racism. The civilisation that is advancing into the 'wilderness' (itself a mythic term suggesting that no culture existed there until Anglo-American society) is always bourgeois white American society. Similarly, the monstrous Other in horror films tends to be anything that threatens the status quo, while the musical and romantic comedy celebrate heteronormative values through their valorisation of the romantic couple.

The complex relation of genre movies to ideology is a matter of debate. On the one hand, genre films are mass-produced fantasies of a culture industry that manipulate us into a false consciousness. From this perspective, their reliance on convention and simplistic plots distract us from awareness of the actual social problems in the real world (see Judith Hess Wright 2003). Yet it is also true that the existence of highly conventional forms allows for the subtle play of irony, parody and appropriation. As Jean-Loup Bourget puts it, the genre film's 'conventionality is the very paradoxical reason for its creativity' (2003: 51).

Popular culture does tend to adhere to dominant ideology, although this is not always the case. Many horror films, melodramas and film noirs, among others, have been shown to question if not subvert accepted values. In a celebrated analysis in the French film journal *Cahiers du cinéma*, published after the tumultuous political events in France in May 1968, Jean

Comolli and Jean Narboni proposed seven possible relations between individual films and their 'textual politics'. Barbara Klinger applies Comolli and Narboni's categories to genre films, focusing on category 'a' films that 'act only as conduits for and perpetuators of existing ideological norms' both in form and content, and category 'e' films, which reveal a tension between style and content, hence problematise their ideological message and thus 'partially dismantle the system from within' (2003: 78). Pam Cook (1976) takes a similar view of B movies and exploitation films, arguing that their production values, less sophisticated than mainstream Hollywood movies, are more readily perceived by viewers as representations, hence allowing for a more critical viewing position.

Often genre movies are conflicted in their ideological view, their more critical aspirations in tension with the constraints of generic convention. John Carpenter's *They Live* (1988) is a good example. A science fiction film about aliens infiltrating Earth, disguised as humans and living among us, *They Live* ultimately becomes the very kind of popular entertainment that the film begins by critiquing. The aliens, wanting to exploit Earth's resources while keeping humanity pacified, have infiltrated human society and control the media, literally creating what Frankfurt School critics would call a state of false consciousness encoded in a television signal that encourages 'an artificially induced state of consciousness that resembles sleep'. People must wear special sunglasses to become aware of the subtextual messages of the media that exhort us to be happy, to reproduce and to consume – that is, they must see through the surface of cultural texts to decode their ideological messages. Yet the film abandons this view halfway through to become instead an improbable action movie, with its hero, Nada (Roddy Piper), single-handedly destroying the aliens' apparently sole broadcasting station and thus saving the world. Initially attacking the mass media for its distracting fantasies, *They Live* turns into the kind of basic super-hero adventure that drives so much of popular culture. Like *The Running Man* (1987), *They Live* ends up fulfilling the requirements of escapist action even as it condemns the media for providing it.

Dynamics of Genre

Genres are neither static nor fixed. Apart from problems of definition and boundaries, genres are processes that are ongoing. They undergo change over time, each new film and cycle adding to the tradition and modifying it. Some critics describe these changes as evolution, others as development, but both terms carry evaluative connotations. Rick Altman theorises that generic change can be traced by the linguistic pattern wherein the adjectival descriptors of generic names evolve away from their anchoring terms and become stand-alone nouns. His examples include epic poetry, out of which the epic genre emerged, and the musical, which developed from musical comedy (1999: 50–3).

One of the first critics to propose the 'life' of art forms was Henri Focillon, who proposed a trajectory of 'the experimental age, the classic age, the age of refinement, the baroque age' (1942: 10). Some genre critics accept a general pattern of change that moves from an early formative stage through a classical period of archetypal expression to a more intellectual phase in which conventions are examined and questioned rather than merely presented, and finally to an ironic, self-conscious mode typically expressed by parody. Thomas Schatz, for example, argues that genres evolve from 'straightforward storytelling to self-conscious formalism' (1981: 38).

Parody requires viewers literate in generic protocol, for only when audiences are widely familiar with the conventions of particular works or a genre can they be parodied effectively. In Mel Brooks' *Young Frankenstein* (1974), a parody of the 1930s cycle of Universal horror films, the monster (Peter Boyle) comes across a little girl playing by a lake and tosses flowers into the water with her; when there are no more, she innocently asks what they should throw in now. There is a cut to a close-up of the creature looking knowingly at the camera. The connecting gaze between the actor in the story and the film viewer is based on the shared knowledge that in the most well-known version of *Frankenstein* (1931) the monster accidentally drowns the girl by throwing her in the water, naively expecting her to float as well, and triggering the wrath of the villagers. In *Young Frankenstein* the joke is based on the disparity between the innocence of the girl's question in relation to the generic knowledge of both the viewer and (improbably) the character.

However, generic phases do not fall into convenient chronological and progressive periods, but often overlap significantly. For some, the western evolved from the supposed classicism of *Stagecoach* to the end of the intellectual trail with *The Wild Bunch* (1969) just thirty years later, and then Brooks' *Blazing Saddles* marking the end of the classic western and the beginning of the parody or baroque phase. But the western was already parodied even before this intellectual period in such films as Buster Keaton's *Go West* (1925), *Destry Rides Again* (1932, 1939) and the Marx Brothers' *Go West* (1940). Looking closely at silent-era westerns and at the implicit assumptions of several important genre critics, Tag Gallagher concludes that, contrary to their shared view, there is no evidence that film genres evolve towards greater embellishment and elaboration. He cites, for example, the scene in *Rio Bravo* where a wounded villain's hiding place on the upper floor of the saloon is revealed by blood dripping down, but points out that the same device was used by John Ford in *The Scarlet Drop* (1918) decades earlier, and even then dismissed by critics as 'old hat' (2003: 266). Gallagher insists instead that even 'a superficial glance at film history suggests cyclicism rather than evolution' (2003: 268).

Genre history, at least, does seem to be shaped to a significant degree by cycles, relatively brief but intense periods of production of a similar group of genre movies. For example, during the 1950s surge in science fiction film production, after the success of *The Incredible Shrinking Man* (1957), there was, in short order, *The Amazing Colossal Man* (1957), *Attack of the 50 Foot Woman* (1958) and *Attack of the Puppet People* (1958) – all movies that used special effects to exploit the disparities of scale.

The detective film in the 1930s was dominated by a cycle of Oriental detective films and series, spurred by the popularity of the *Charlie Chan* series that began with *Charlie Chan Carries On* in 1931. A number of actors (none of whom were Chinese) played Chan in over two dozen films produced first by Fox and then by Monogram studios until the series finally ended in 1947. Twentieth Century Fox sought to cash in on the success of the Chan films with its *Mr. Moto* series, starring Peter Lorre as the eponymous Japanese detective, and Monogram also responded with its *Mr. Wong* films featuring Boris Karloff. Combining stereotypes of Oriental characters with the detective or mystery format, the cycle was brought largely to a halt by the outbreak of World War Two and the retooling of Asian stereotypes as enemies in war films. Altman (1999) suggests that cycles are distinguishable from subgenres in that while a subgenre can be shared among different studios, cycles tend to be 'proprietary', dominated by a particular studio, as in the case of the Warner Bros. biopics in the 1930s that began with *Disraeli* (1929). However, this claim is questionable, particularly after the decline of the studio system. More recently, the big box office success of the action movie *Speed* (1994, Twentieth Century Fox), with a kinetic plot involving a bomb on a bus that cannot stop or it will explode, was followed by *Money Train* (1995, Columbia) and *Broken Arrow* (1996, Twentieth Century Fox) with runaway trains, and *Swordfish* (2001, Warner Bros.) with its airborne bus hauled by a helicopter. *Rumble in the Bronx* (*Hong Faan Kui*, 1996, Golden Harvest/New Line Cinema), with a runaway hovercraft, was made in and produced with funding from Canada and Hong Kong, showing the ability of cycles to work not only among studios but also across nations.

John Cawelti has argued that there were particularly profound changes in American genre movies in the 1970s across all genres. Aware of themselves as myth, genre movies of the period responded in four ways: humorous burlesque, nostalgia, demythologisation and reaffirmation (2003: 243). This development was the result in part of the demise of the Hays Office in 1967 and the continuing break-up of the traditional studio system, allowing directors greater freedom in a more disillusioned and cynical era. Also, the popularisation of the auteur theory (discussed in the next chapter) permitted the generation of 'movie brats' – younger directors such as Martin Scorsese, Steven Spielberg, Robert Altman, Francis Ford Coppola, Brian de Palma and John Carpenter – to make genre films by choice rather than assignment. Films like Coppola's *The Godfather* (1972) and *Apocalypse Now* (1979), Scorsese's *Mean Streets* (1973) and *New York, New York* (1977), Altman's *McCabe and Mrs. Miller*, *The Long Goodbye* and *Nashville* (1975), and de Palma's *Sisters* (1973), *Phantom of the Paradise* (1975) and *Obsession* (1976) are genre movies by directors who had grown up watching genre movies on television and studying them in academic film programmes. With a more contemporary sensibility, these filmmakers inevitably made genre films that were at once burdened and liberated by an awareness of generic myth.

For Cawelti, the changes in the period's genre films were so profound that he wondered whether the traditional film genres had exhausted themselves and hypothesised that 'the cultural myths they once embodied are no longer fully adequate to the imaginative needs of our time' (2003: 260). Certainly at different historical moments, different genres are received differently and have different degrees of popularity. As Leo Braudy explains:

Genre films essentially ask the audience, 'Do you still want to believe this?' Popularity is the audience answering, 'Yes.' Change in genres occurs when the audience says, 'That's too infantile a form of what we believe. Show us something more complicated.' (1977: 179)

The shifting fortune of the western is perhaps the most dramatic example of changing audience acceptance. Once the mainstay of Hollywood studio production, the genre declined precipitously after the revisionist and parody westerns of the 1970s. In the post-Vietnam era westerns no longer seemed able to offer the kind of appeal they once did. For example, given the compromised wars and botched operations that have characterised the American military since Korea, viewers have doubted the efficacy of their armed forces, and so found it difficult to accept without irony conventions such as the cavalry coming decisively to the rescue – as in *Stagecoach*, when the platoon appears in the nick of time to save the day.

While George Bush was able to invoke the rhetoric of the western to bolster domestic support for his war on terrorism, contemporary viewers tend to snigger at the convenient appearance of the cavalry in *Stagecoach*. However, essentially the same convention enthrals spectators watching Han Solo (Harrison Ford) come back for the final showdown with the Death Star in *Star Wars* (1977). George Lucas' adaptation of genre conventions for his blockbuster space adventure marked the beginning of science fiction's usurpation of the western in the popular imagination. Indeed, many science fiction movies are like westerns, with space becoming, in the famous words of *Star Trek*'s opening voice-over, the 'final frontier'. In the lawless expanse of space, heroes and villains wield laser guns instead of sixguns, space cowboys jockey customised rockets instead of riding horses, and aliens – as a movie like *Alien Nation* (1988) makes explicit – serve as the swarthy Other in the place of Indians. In *Star Wars*, Lucas designed the scene where Luke Skywalker (Mark Hamill) finds his aunt and uncle killed and their homestead destroyed by storm troopers as an homage to the scene in *The Searchers* (1956) when Ethan Edwards (John Wayne) discovers the charred and defiled bodies of his brother's family after an Indian attack. Subsequently, there appeared a cycle of science fiction adaptations of famous westerns, including *Enemy Mine* (1985), a remake of *Broken Arrow* (1950); *Outland* (1981), a version of *High Noon*

(1952) set on a space mining station instead of a frontier town; and *Battle Beyond the Stars* (1980), a remake of *The Magnificent Seven* (1960), itself a remake of Akira Kurosawa's *The Seven Samurai* (1954).

The western myth survives within a different genre, one with a technological iconography rather than a pastoral one, perhaps because it is more related to our daily experience. Originally westerns appealed to audiences at a time when modernity was eliminating the frontier; now, because we are more likely to be familiar with computers than horses, and more likely to visit the new frontier of cyberspace than what remains of the wilderness, the classic western has been largely replaced by the science fiction film. Altman suggests that genres are composed of both semantic and syntactic elements – roughly distinguishing iconography and conventions from themes and narrative structures, or outer and inner form – and cites the western as one of the genres that has proven most 'durable' because it has 'established the most coherent syntax' (1999: 225). The successful transformation of the western into the imagery of science fiction would seem to be a case in point.

Case Study: The Musical – 42nd Street and Pennies from Heaven

The musical genre developed quickly after the arrival of sound in 1927. Warner Bros. particularly took the early lead with its Vitaphone system for producing synchronised sound, and released the first all-talking feature, *The Jazz Singer*, in 1927. By the early 1930s the studio had produced a remarkable cycle of musicals, many featuring the choreography of Busby Berkeley, including *Golddiggers of 1933*, *Footlight Parade* and *42nd Street* (all 1933). With their upbeat messages of group effort and success, as well as their visual lavishness offering a stark contrast to the realities of economic impoverishment, these musicals were very popular with Depression-era audiences.

While films of every genre employ a romantic subplot, an overwhelming number of musicals are constructed around romance. On one level, the connection between music and romance is hardly surprising, given Western culture's valorisation of music as the medium that speaks to the soul or heart, and consequently pop music's emphasis on love as its dominant subject. Often, the romantic plot involves a developing attraction and comic misunderstanding between the protagonists that is eventually resolved with the couple getting together in marriage or its promise. This is the essential plot of numerous musicals, from the RKO cycle with Fred Astaire and Ginger Rogers in the 1930s, to *West Side Story* and *Moulin Rouge!* (2001). In *On the Town* three sailors manage to find their true loves while on a one-day pass in New York City, and the narrative resolution of *Seven Brides for Seven Brothers* (1954) is evident from its title.

The idealised representation of sexual desire as heterosexual romance and union is one of the mythic and ideological functions of much popular culture, including the musical. Dance, in which the partners move in harmonious physical rhythms, has served as a ready sexual metaphor at least since hot dance jazz of the 1920s. As Ginger sings to Fred in 'The Continental' number in *The Gay Divorcee* (1934), 'You tell of your love while you dance'. In the Astaire/Rogers films, their union in the narrative is invariably signalled by a final dance in celebration of their reconciliation. In *The Pirate* (1948), Gene Kelly, known as a more 'virile' dancer than Astaire, sings the song 'Niña', a proclamation of his sexual prowess and indiscriminate love for all women, while dancing with bold, athletic gestures as he climbs up balconies and around various balustrades and poles, the *mise-en-scène* a riot of phallic imagery – even ending with a smoking cigarette popping out of his mouth – in a scene that makes particularly explicit the sexual subtext of song and dance. Musical performance provides a conventionalised way of addressing issues of sexuality indirectly, in a manner suitable to both audiences and the Hays Office. From the show's cast in *The Band Wagon* to the New York street gangs of *West Side Story* to the female prison inmates in *Chicago* (2002), groups in musicals that sing and dance together express communal solidarity. The transformation of desire into romance tames any potential threat to the larger social community.

The first production number in *42nd Street*, 'Shuffle Off to Buffalo', acknowledges the obligatory romantic union between Peggy (Ruby Keeler) and juvenile Billy Lawler (Dick Powell), but the union in *42nd Street* is not only that of the romantic couple, but the larger union of the nation itself. The film's main plot concerns the attempt of legendary Broadway director Julian Marsh (Warner Baxter) to mount a new musical show, 'Pretty Lady', despite the economic difficulties of the Depression and internecine and personal problems among the cast and crew. Marsh himself has lost everything in the stock market crash and tells his producers that he has agreed to direct the show 'for only one reason – money. It's got to support

Figure 4 *42nd Street*: everyone works to put on the show

me for a long time'. Petty politics and personal interest motivate many of the characters involved in the production, but when several crises develop as opening night approaches, the characters all sacrifice their personal concerns in order for the show to go on.

In *42nd Street*, as in *Golddiggers of 1933* and *Footlight Parade*, the story concludes that everyone has to pull together to mount the show. The opening number of *Golddiggers of 1933*, 'We're in the Money', makes clear the metaphoric connection between theatrical show and the economy, as the chorines, dressed in costumes representing coins and singing about being financially flush, are interrupted by men from the sheriff's office repossessing the costumes, sets and equipment because the producer has not paid his bills. In *42nd Street*, similarly, the show that must be put on is both a musical and a business enterprise. Everyone talks about the fact that the show represents an investment by entrepreneur Abner Dillon (Guy Kibee), who is hoping to date a chorus girl as his return. The beginning of rehearsals is a clash of egos and personal concerns, and the aspiring chorus girls push each other, jockeying for position on the audition line. But when temperamental star Dorothy Brock (Bebe Daniels) dumps Abner after rehearsals begin, and the show is in danger of folding before it opens, Abner agrees to let the show go on; while Dorothy, initially angry and jealous after being replaced by newcomer Peggy Sawyer, instead gives Peggy a stirring speech of encouragement before Peggy goes on stage as her replacement after Dorothy falls and breaks her ankle. And, too, there is Marsh's stirring speech to Peggy as she makes her debut: 'Two hundred people, two hundred jobs, two hundred thousand dollars, five weeks of grind and blood and sweat depend upon you … and, Sawyer, you're going out a youngster, but you've got to come back a star!'

Upon agreeing to direct the show, Marsh learns that he has a heart problem and is seriously ill. As he proceeds to whip his cast into shape, rehearsing them night and day in order to open in five weeks, he is visibly ailing but carries on anyway. Physically and financially, he is in a weakened state. But he is nevertheless a strong and paternal leader who will sacrifice himself for the good of all, if necessary. In rehearsals before the show opens, Marsh emphasises the importance of teamwork and discipline ('you're going to work, sweat and work some more') in order to make the show a success. At the end of the film, when the show has concluded its successful debut and the satisfied patrons are leaving the theatre, the final shot shows Marsh, alone after everyone departs, the exhausted leader who has ensured another triumph.

The production numbers within the 'Pretty Lady' show offered a lavish spectacle that appealed to Depression audiences. Importantly, no stage production could ever hope to achieve the kind of elaborate spectacles supposedly taking place on a theatre stage in *42nd Street*. Berkeley's production numbers are made for film viewers, not theatre spectators. The camera moves freely from the perspective of the theatre audience in the story to bird's-eye views of the dancers, creating visual patterns that sway and reconfigure, and which could be appreciated only from above. The film also uses other cinematic as opposed to stage techniques to create its opulent spectacles. When Peggy and Billy kiss in the 'Shuffle Off to Buffalo' number, the chorines appear suddenly behind them as a result of film editing, not stagecraft. At the conclusion of the number the camera tracks through the spread legs of the chorines, a perspective unavailable to the audience in the film supposedly watching this performance. In the climactic number, the eponymous '42nd Street', there is a cut from Peggy singing and tapping a solo on the roof of an automobile to an elaborate street *mise-en-scène* that was not there in the shots before.

Berkeley's production numbers are perfectly suited to the theme of the story. Just as the characters must pull together for their mutual effort to succeed, so all the chorines in the production numbers have to perform in synchronisation for the visual effects to work. Emphasising the importance of geometric patterns and shapes, Berkeley's drill team-like dance routines, as with the 'Pretty Lady' show itself, require both individual and group effort. Thus, both the genre's backstage narrative and the musical numbers present a message of group unity. In the film's historical context, the show that must be, and is, successfully put on becomes a metaphor for getting the country 'back on its feet'. Peggy's successful rise to stardom is a variation of the Horatio Alger success story of rising to the top through pluck and luck; also, in putting on the show, the dancers' vitality of motion might be said to equal the dynamic energy of the American spirit, and the lavishness of the production numbers themselves an affirmation of the American Dream.

***

The Golden Age of the Hollywood musical is generally considered the 1950s, when many musicals, particularly those produced by MGM's Freed Unit (named for producer Arthur Freed), grew more sophisticated in integrating plots and musical sequences. In *It's Always Fair Weather* (1955), for example, sparring smoothly segues into choreography in the 'Stillman's Gym' number, and the 'Situation Wise' number grows organically out of the verbal rhythms of the advertising executives' jargon. Yet only a decade later the production of musicals in Hollywood dropped drastically. The downturn in big-budget musicals during this period can be linked to the widening gap between the kind of music used in the musicals that the studios were producing and the music that an increasing percentage of the movie-going audience was actually listening to – rock 'n' roll (Grant 1986).

The Girl Can't Help It (1956), the first big-budget Hollywood musical with rock music, contains a prologue in which star Tom Ewell appears as 'himself' and, speaking directly to the camera, explains that the film we are about to see is a story about music – 'not the music of long ago, but the music that expresses the culture, the refinement, the polite grace of the present day'. On the word 'culture', the camera pans right to bring a jukebox into centre frame with Ewell; at the end of the sentence, Little

Richard's raucous title tune begins on the soundtrack and the camera tracks into the jukebox, which glows with a red-hot intensity. The song overwhelms the more sedate classical music that precedes it on the soundtrack, as well as Ewell's adult, authoritative narrator. This pre-credit sequence of *The Girl Can't Help It* is a telling expression of the generation gap engendered by the new post-war youth culture of the 1950s. Little Richard's title song refers to the hypersexualised Jerri Jordan (Jayne Mansfield), who causes the milkman's bottles to pop open and overflow when he sees her walking down the street. The association of rock music with sexuality and unleashed libido seemed antithetical to the romantic and communal syntax of the Hollywood musical, but as the trajectory of Elvis Presley's film career shows, the genre was able to absorb and defuse rock music of its more primal connotations.

Pennies from Heaven (1981) is a refined or intellectual stage musical that, in its awareness of popular music's sexual ideology, could exist only after rock 'n' roll. The film professes a more frank view about desire than ever expressed directly by earlier popular music, yet does so by using that very music in sometimes wildly inappropriate contexts. Most obviously, characters sing male and female parts regardless of their gender. The songs are all actual recordings of 1930s popular vocalists like Connie Boswell, Bing Crosby and Rudy Vallee, with the actors lip-synching. This postmodern juxtaposition, which shatters the illusion of the musical's utopian plentitude, is central to the film's theme, the influence of pop culture on our individual and collective consciousness.

The film's plot involves Arthur (Steve Martin), a sheet music salesman who believes fervently in the American Dream. Living in a stultifying marriage with his wife Joan (Jessica Harper), Arthur falls for and seduces a schoolteacher, Eileen (Bernadette Peters). Becoming pregnant, Eileen loses her job, leaves home and becomes a prostitute in order to survive. Arthur spends his wife's inheritance on a record shop, but the business fails and, meeting Eileen again by chance, they decide to leave town together. Circumstantial evidence causes Arthur to be arrested, convicted and sentenced to death for the murder of a blind girl. The ending is somewhat ambiguous but Arthur's inexplicable happy reunion with Eileen after being led to the gallows may be understood as his final (dying?) fantasy, yet another determined by Arthur's belief in the romantic vision of the pop songs he had sold.

A salesman, Arthur, ironically, has himself been 'sold' on the sunny ideology of Depression-era pop music – the impossibly optimistic view that every cloud has a silver lining and that every time it rains, it rains pennies from heaven. Embracing, like the title song, a staunchly upbeat perspective, Arthur's imagination transforms an itinerant musician, known as Accordian Player (Vernel Bagneris), from an awkward stutterer to an eloquently expressive dancer, his cloying subservience now the fluid dance of a free spirit in the title number. When the sequence begins, the roadside café where the two men are eating opens up like the Pullman Porter in *42nd Street*, but only Arthur notices.

A fervent romantic, Arthur imagines the production number 'Did You Ever See a Dream Walking?' when he first sees Eileen in a music shop. Later, Arthur and Eileen go to the cinema, where they watch Astaire and Rogers in *Follow the Fleet* (1936). Arthur becomes transfixed by the film couple's romantic allure, and he and Eileen appear on the stage beneath the screen, dancing in perfect harmony with the towering images of Fred and Ginger in the 'Let's Face the Music and Dance' number (the lyrics taking on a more ominous undertone for Arthur, who is soon to be arrested). Then, suddenly, Arthur and Eileen are 'in' the number, as Fred and Ginger, in a marvellous reconstruction of the original scene that suggests the way we project ourselves into the fantasy worlds of movies (and as Arthur also does with song).

If earlier Hollywood musicals sought to integrate story and production numbers into a unified work, *Pennies from Heaven* emphasises dissonance between narrative and music. Most obviously, the voices are only lip-synched, not the voices of the actors on screen. (Ironically, this gives *Pennies from Heaven* a greater truth than most musicals, in which the actors lip-synch their voices – or someone else's – with the sound recorded at another time and mixed in later.) The production numbers are all contextualised as fantasies of the characters, and the film's plot emphasises the disparity between pop culture fantasies and the harsh realities of Arthur's noirish world. When, for example, the bank manager refuses Arthur a loan to start his business because he has no collateral, suddenly the musical sequence 'Yes, Yes' ('My Baby Said Yes, Yes Instead of No, No') begins. The song's insistent positivism is a denial of Arthur's rejection by the banker, and the choreography includes the two of them happily dancing together along with a line of tellers cheerfully bestowing sacks of money upon

Figure 5 *Pennies from Heaven*: yes, yes, instead of no, no

Arthur. At the end of the sequence we see Arthur in his car, riding home dejectedly after being denied a loan at the bank.

Arthur insists that 'songs tell the truth', but life as envisioned by *Pennies from Heaven* is hardly the romantic fantasy offered by the Astaire-Rogers musicals. A billboard advertising a movie entitled 'Love before Breakfast' looms in the background by the bridge where several fateful events take place in the story for Arthur, but Arthur's marriage is loveless at any time of day – or night. While in earlier musicals singing and dancing tends to express love and joy, Joan sings 'It's a Sin to Tell a Lie' in response to her cheating husband, making Dolly Dawn's original vocal sound much more ominous while imagining stabbing Arthur in the back with a pair of scissors. At the nadir of Arthur's relationship with Eileen, the couple are in a seedy hotel room, Arthur wearing a T-shirt like Burt Lancaster in *The Killers* (1946) and *I Walk Alone* (1948), the hotel's neon marquee blinking on and off. The *mise-en-scène* here, borrowed from film noir, stands in stark opposition to Arthur's brightly-lit musical fantasies.

The disjunction between Arthur's imagination and the real world shows how torn Arthur is between his own animal desire and the romantic visions of popular song. Arthur vacillates between idolising Eileen and regarding her as a sex object. Not knowing how to distinguish his fantasy from reality, Arthur is in a way as blind as the blind girl he meets, tellingly, in a tunnel. Measured against the classic musicals of the 1930s–1950s, *Pennies from Heaven* might be described as an anti-musical, but that is only because it works oppositely from classical musicals. If musicals conventionally use musical numbers as fantasies of sublimated desire, *Pennies from Heaven* employs its music to reveal how the fantasies of popular music do so. The film's unconventional staging of its musical numbers distances viewers, preventing them from escaping into the musical's typically appealing illusionary world as Arthur, the model cultural dupe, escapes into popular song.

Case Study: The Horror Film – Invasion of the Body Snatchers and Night of the Living Dead

Apart from the western, there has been more written about the horror film than any other genre. Of all this work, undoubtedly the most influential has been that of Robin Wood. Combining aspects of Marxist, psychoanalytic, feminist and structural analysis, Wood proposes an elegantly simple dramatic structure as the core of the genre: they are 'our collective nightmares … in which normality is threatened by a monster' (1979b: 10). He sees the genre as an articulation of the Freudian notion of the return of the repressed: that is, the horror film expresses cultural and ideological contradictions that otherwise we deny. For Wood, the subject of horror is 'the struggle for recognition of all that our civilisation *re*presses or *op*presses'. The source of horror, the monster, is thus the Other in the sense used by Barthes: that which we cannot admit of ourselves and so disavow by projecting outward, onto another. Wood provides a list of specific Others in the horror genre: women, the proletariat, other cultures, ethnic groups, alternative ideologies or political systems, children and deviations from sexual norms (1979b: 9–11). All of these have been taken up by critics of the genre over the last three decades, although the last category – deviations from sexual norms – has been the one most frequently explored.

Wood's usefully concise definition allows him to identify horror's primary binary opposition as one between the monstrous and the normal, and to suggest that the ideological position in any given horror film is expressed by the relation between these two terms. It is in this relation that each horror film defines what is 'normal' and what is 'monstrous'. Broadly speaking, conservative films endorse the ideological status quo, literally demonising deviations from the norm as monstrous; by contrast, progressive examples of the genre challenge these values, either by making the creature sympathetic or by showing normal society to be in some way horrifying in itself, problematising any easy distinction between normal and monstrous.

Most horror films are consistent in defining normality as the heterosexual, monogamous couple, the family, and the social institutions (police, church, military) that support and defend them. The monster in these films is a projection of the dominant ideology's anxiety about itself and its continuation, but disguised as a grotesque other – what Wood calls the inevitable 'return of the repressed'. Many horror movies tend to allow spectators the pleasure of identifying with the monster's status as outsider, but ultimately contain any potentially subversive response by having the monster defeated by characters representative of social authority. In the terms of one of the genre's conventions for expressing this ideological dynamic, victorious human heroes gaze at the destroyed remains of the monster and ruminate with seeming profundity that there are certain things that man is not meant to know.

In Bram Stoker's novel *Dracula* (1897), the vampiric Count clearly represents an unleashed sexuality that was strongly repressed during the Victorian era, when the novel was published. Subsequent film variations of the vampire have accommodated a wide range of interpretations, including fascism (*Mark of the Vampire*, 1944), Marxism (*Andy Warhol's Dracula*, aka *Blood for Dracula*, 1974) and race (*Blacula*, 1972; *Vampire in Brooklyn*, 1995). But it is the sexual aspect, whether in the buxom victims of Hammer Studio's *Horror of Dracula* (1958), the seductive romanticism of Frank Langella's *Dracula* (1979) or the lesbian vampire movies like *Daughters of Darkness* (1971) and *The Velvet Vampire* (1971), that has been the dominant preoccupation of vampire movies.

This is the emphasis, for example, of the most famous of vampire movies, Tod Browning's *Dracula* (1931). The film, based on the play (1927), in turn based on the novel (1897), today seems rather stage-bound, the special effects unconvincing (in his bat form, Dracula never seems more than a rubber toy dangling on a wire), and much of the action, including the climactic death of the vampire, takes place off-screen. Its vision of the normal, the monstrous and their relation is equally as schematic, but Bela Lugosi's incarnation of the undead Count in *Dracula*, first on stage and then in Universal's classic film, has become the familiar icon of the movie vampire. Dracula's foreign accent, along with his aristocratic bearing and title, renders him as Other, a more monstrous version of the lustful nobleman familiar from English literature since Samuel Richardson's *Pamela* (1740).

In the plot, after an eerie ride through the Carpathian mountains in eastern Europe, Renfield (Dwight Frye) arrives at castle Dracula to complete a London real estate deal with Count Dracula. Renfield is turned into one of Dracula's thralls, protecting him during his sea voyage to London, where upon arrival Dracula attacks young Lucy Weston (Frances Dade), turning her into a vampire. Dracula is a sexual seducer who slips by night into young women's boudoirs and transports them with his erotic kisses. When Dracula next turns to Lucy's friend Mina (Helen Chandler), her father calls in a specialist, Dr Abraham Van Helsing (Edward Van Sloan), who deduces that the mysterious Count is in fact a vampire. In the film's climax, Van Helsing, with the help of Mina's fiancé, John Harker (David Manners), tracks Dracula to his lair and destroys him.

In *Dracula* Van Helsing, far from the superhero makeover he received for *Van Helsing* (2004), is a benevolent figure of paternal patriarchy. A man of science, he uses deductive logic to determine that a vampire is at work, and combines it with action, enlisting the young hero Harker to help him destroy the threat of the vampire, tracking him to his own lair. The creature is destroyed and phallic sexuality staked in favour of monogamous hetero-sexuality. In the film's final shot, with Dracula now finally able to rest in peace, the young couple ascend a long staircase to the heavenly light of day, accompanied by the promise of wedding bells on the soundtrack as the final fade-out suggests they will live happily ever after.

***

Invasion of the Body Snatchers (1956), like *Dracula*, also raises issues about women and their growing independence, but the film's focus is more on contemporary social and political concerns. By the 1950s, the real and potential horrors of the nuclear age and Cold War anxieties made Stoker's middle-European Count seem somewhat dated. Recalling Cawelti's discussion of 1970s genre films, Wood suggests that in today's more sexually liberal society the conventional vampire should be discarded as an anachronism (1996: 378). Many movie vampires have appeared since 1983 when Wood originally urged that the undead Count be allowed to rest in peace, but more appropriate to the terror of potential nuclear and biological annihilation are apocalyptic visions of undead legions, as in *Invasion of the Body Snatchers* and *Night of the Living Dead*. These horror films exploit Stoker's association of Dracula with the plague or contagion (shown in *Nosferatu* (1922), but not in *Dracula*), but imagine the infection on a national rather than personal scale. In *Invasion of the Body Snatchers*, all of society is threatened with emotionless replicas, zombie duplicates that, like vampires, consume our minds, bodies and souls. At a time when Americans felt particularly threatened both from within and without, the film offered a horrific yet ambiguous metaphor of the monstrous as both communist infiltration and creeping conformism.

The story is told in flashback by a wildly dishevelled doctor, Miles Bennell (Kevin McCarthy), to another doctor and a psychiatrist in a hospital emergency room. Dr Bennell explains that upon returning home from a conference to his small town of Santa Mira, he stumbled upon what at first seemed a strange mass delusion whereby people were having paranoid fantasies that their friends or family members were imposters. His old flame Becky (Dana Wynter), now divorced, returns to town and they go out on a date for dinner, but are interrupted when his friends Jack (King Donovan) and Teddy (Carolyn Jones) telephone, urging Miles to come to their house, where they find a mysterious, half-formed body that bears an uncomfortable resemblance to Jack. The next morning the two couples discover replicant bodies of themselves popping out of large pods in Miles' greenhouse. Splitting up, the couples try to escape, but Miles and Becky end up doubling back and hiding in his office. The following day Jack, now a pod person, shows up with other pod replacements to detain Miles and Becky until they fall asleep. The two manage to escape and hide out from the pursuing townsfolk in an abandoned mine shaft, but Becky falls asleep, becomes a pod, and alerts the entire town to Miles' whereabouts. He flees to a nearby highway, where he stands between lanes jammed with traffic shouting warnings ('You're next!') to the heedless drivers and directly to the camera before a fade-out returns us to the present, where Miles has been telling his story in the hospital.

Director Don Siegel wanted to end the film here, but Allied Artists forced him to add the narrative frame that makes the story a flashback. In the

Figure 6 *Invasion of the Body Snatchers*: alien pods threaten domestic space

added ending, Miles finishes telling his story, convincing his listeners only of his insanity, but at the last minute an injured truck driver is wheeled in for surgery as the paramedics explain that he was coming from Santa Mira and was buried under some weird looking pods. Now believing Miles, the psychiatrist (Whit Bissell) instructs the staff to get the FBI and the President on the telephone. This imposed ending may seem upbeat, but in fact does not provide the comfortable closure of a horror movie like *Dracula*. For how could the FBI or anyone possibly contain the pod invasion, which by now has spread much wider than the town of Santa Mira? The film's ending is considerably more ambiguous than the ending of Jack Finney's source novel, in which Miles sets fire to a field of growing pods, forcing those that do not burn to rise into the sky and retreat from Earth.

The ambiguity of the film's ending is indicative of its ambivalence towards the normal and monstrous. The pod people are a horrific, emotion-less Other bent on destroying humanity. Like the giant ants in *Them!* (1954), the emotionless pod people ('No more love, no more beauty, no more pain') work for a collectivist mentality that threatens to undermine America.

The pod people gather in the town square, brought together by some silent signal, to spread the conspiracy by taking pods to nearby towns and cities. Yet at the same time, the pod people are only horrific exaggerations of the alienation of modern American life: as Miles observes while hiding in his office, 'In my practice I've seen how people have allowed their humanity to drain away … We harden our hearts. Grow callous.' In the climax, everyone in town pursues Miles and Becky up the long stairway into the hills as the town warning siren blasts ominously. The crowd searches out dissenters like Miles, recalling the HUAC witch hunts of a few years earlier. The relative proximity of the highway, when Miles finally reaches it, provides an extra horrific twist by enacting this nightmarish invasion so close to the flow of civilisation. The cars are bumper-to-bumper, the drivers oblivious to what is going on around them, already alienated in their rush to nowhere.

The film makes the mundane seem menacing, as in the scene where Miles and Becky visit her cousin Wilma (Virginia Christine), who is convinced that her Uncle Ira is no longer her Uncle Ira. Nothing dramatic happens, but Ira is shown in a slightly canted image, suggesting that something is off kilter as he goes through the banal motions of mowing the lawn and chatting idly about the weather. Even before *Psycho*, *Invasion of the Body Snatchers* revealed the horrors of the quotidian world. The film begins in sunny southern California but grows darker and more threatening, a movement paralleled by the increasingly smaller spaces in which the characters are placed, from Becky's basement to the closet in Miles' office to the hole in the ground in the mineshaft. The image of Miles and Becky running down an alley in the dark of night, looking for a place to hide, evokes such classic 'outlaw couple' noirs as *You Only Live Once* (1937) and *They Drive by Night* (1949). As in *It's a Wonderful Life*, the town changes from a Norman Rockwell vision of idyllic small-town America to a noirish nightmare.

***

Drake Douglas explains the derivation and the original power of the zombie, the only important movie monster of legendary proportion to emerge from the New World, as a horrifying image for enslaved blacks in America and their consequent loss of volition in perpetuity (Douglas 1969: 158–71). This meaning is invoked in the first important zombie movie, *White Zombie* (1932), when one of the undead workers is crushed by the grinding apparatus of a sugar mill as the rest unflinchingly carry on with their tasks, grist for the mill of capitalist exploitation. More contemporary zombies have figured as metaphors of modern crowd behaviour (Waller 1986: 279), a direction initiated by George A. Romero's *Night of the Living Dead* in 1968 and taken to comic extreme in *Shaun of the Dead* (2004) and *Fido* (2006). *Night of the Living Dead* reverses many conventions of the genre and, perhaps because it was made independently, outside of Hollywood, boldly depicts normality itself as unambiguously monstrous. Romero's independently-produced film has been extraordinarily influential within the horror genre, spawning three sequels (*Dawn of the Dead*, 1978; *Day of the Dead*, 1985; and *Land of the Dead*, 2005), numerous imitations and establishing a new monster mythology.

Night of the Living Dead begins with brother and sister Johnny (Russell Streiner) and Barbara (Judith O'Dea) driving in their car for an obligatory visit to their father's grave in a rural cemetery. Suddenly they are attacked by a ghoulish figure in the graveyard. Johnny is overwhelmed by the attacker, and in a state of shock Barbara manages to escape to a nearby farmhouse. Soon she is joined by Ben (Duane Jones), also fleeing from the ghouls. After fighting off several zombies and boarding up the doors and windows of the house, they discover several other people hiding in the basement: Harry Cooper (Karl Hardman), his wife Helen (Marilyn Eastman) and young daughter, Karen (Kyra Schon) – who has been bitten by one of the zombies – and a pair of teenage lovebirds, Tom (Keith Wayne) and Judy (Judith Ridley). Harry and Ben disagree over whether to escape or barricade themselves in the basement, eventually trying Ben's plan, but Tom and Judy are killed when the truck they attempt to fill with gas explodes, and their charred remains are consumed by the zombies. Harry thinks only of his family, endangering the others as a result, and in a power struggle and scuffle over a rifle Ben kills him. Karen turns into a zombie, kills her mother and is shot by Ben, who then seals the basement door, preventing the zombies from entering. In the light of morning Ben emerges from the basement, only to be shot by a member of a vigilante group moving through the area trying to clear it of zombies.

The film consistently violates generic convention. Unlike most earlier horror films, in *Night of the Living Dead* the horror begins immediately, and in the daytime rather than at night. The death of the endearing teenage couple violates the conventions of numerous earlier monster movies, such as *The Blob*, where the young couple live to warn adult civilisation. Ironically, the basement turns out to be the safest place rather than a metaphor for the subconscious terrain from which monsters usually emerge, as in *Psycho*. *Night of the Living Dead* features the conventional scenes of conferences between the military and scientists as civilisation marshals its forces against the monstrous threat, but here the authorities are bumbling, evasive and confused as the news camera vainly pursues them for information. Untypically, the hero is black, which gives the tension between Harry and Ben added resonance. Although the newscast on the farmhouse television suggests a possible explanation for the zombie phenomenon (radiation brought back to Earth from a space probe is reanimating the corpses of the recently deceased), no definitive explanation is ever provided, and ultimately the various institutions (social, religious, military) that defeat the monster in earlier horror films offer no such salvation in *Night of the Living Dead*.

Robin Wood argues that cannibalism 'represents the ultimate in possessiveness, hence the logical end of human relations under capitalism' (1979b: 21). From the beginning of the film there is a clear attack on American society: in the first scene Johnny and Barbara are driving through a cemetery with an American flag in the distance, offering at the outset a chilling image of the pervasiveness of death in American culture. Such imagery was particularly resonant in 1968, during the height of the Vietnam War. Instead of the sense of national community and pride for the flag depicted in *Drums Along the Mohawk* (discussed in the next chapter), the America of *Night of the Living Dead* is marked by death. Tellingly, the zombies are dressed like average folk from all walks of life – that is, middle America. As represented by the bellicose Harry Cooper, the film also attacks the nuclear family, the very institution valorised in the happy ending in *Dracula*.

When, in the end, the sheriff's marksman shoots Ben, it would seem that they cannot tell for sure whether the figure in the house is alive or undead. This is a troubling ambiguity, given that Ben is black and that the vigilante group seem like stereotyped rednecks. The film was made during a period of violent racial tensions in America in the late 1960s. Its grainy black-and-white imagery may have been the result of the film's rather small budget compared to the typical Hollywood feature; however, it adds to the film's power by evoking a *cinéma vérité*-like realism similar to contemporary television news footage of combat in Vietnam and civil rights strife at home. Because the hero is black, the final montage of still images of Ben's body being thrown on a large pyre, his body handled with meathooks, suggests news photos of beatings and lynchings in the American south at the height of the Civil Rights movement. The sheriff's comment, 'another one for the fire', resonates with the fear of racial violence that had erupted in many American cities around the time of the film's release. Whereas an earlier horror movie like *Dracula* presents the normal as unquestionably good and just, and the vampire unwaveringly evil, *Night of the Living Dead* shows normal society (those on the 'inside') as monstrous and as much of a threat as the zombies on the outside.

3   GENRE AND AUTHORSHIP

The Auteur Theory

In the studio era directors were employees, like the other members of a film's cast and crew. Even those few directors who wielded some degree of clout in Hollywood, like Frank Capra and Alfred Hitchcock, had to work within the parameters of the producing studio's dominant style or genre. In the Hollywood studio system, directors, like actors and electricians, were under contract; rarely did they have the right to final cut. Yet while some directors floundered against the pressures of the studio system, many in fact flourished, using the rules of genre as convenience rather than constraint, as guidelines from which to deviate or deepen rather than blueprints to follow.

By providing the received framework of genre, Hollywood gave film-makers a flexible tradition within which to work. Some directors developed their vision within particular genres, such as Samuel Fuller with the war film, John Ford with the western and Douglas Sirk with the melodrama. The auteur approach provided a way of looking at directors' style foregrounded against the background of genre. As Lawrence Alloway notes, 'the personal contribution of many directors can only be seen fully after typical icono-graphical elements have been identified' (1971: 41).

Auteurism, the examination of films by the same director for a consistent personal vision, began in the mid-1950s in the film journal *Cahiers du cinéma*. Critics writing for the magazine, many aspiring to be directors themselves, tended to look at and favour films that could be understood as expressing an authorial viewpoint on the part of the director. Their rallying call was provided in a number of articles written by François Truffaut, then a young critic writing for the magazine. Truffaut launched an attack on the French 'Tradition of Quality', big studio films adapted by writers from literary works popular at the time, arguing that such films were impersonal because they left little room for the director. In the polemical 1954 article 'La Politique des Auteurs', Truffaut argued that a more artistic and truly cinematic style of filmmaking could be achieved with smaller budgets and a more personal approach to production. For many of the *Cahiers* writers, the auteur approach became a critical practice of discovering a worldview, a philosophy, across a number of texts by one director by looking for stylistic and thematic connections from film to film. Auteurs are perceived through a basic pattern of repeated themes and motifs (Nowell-Smith 1968: 10).

Although *Cahiers* writers paid attention to European art cinema directors, they focused on Hollywood – a provocative gesture given Hollywood's studio system and its emphasis on entertainment rather than art. It is not surprising that when many of these critics eventually did become directors, they often made films that were takes on genre films: Truffaut's *Tirez sur le pianiste* (*Shoot the Piano Player*, 1960) winks at crime films and thrillers, and *La Peau Douce* (*The Soft Skin*, 1964) is a domestic melodrama; Claude Chabrol's many thrillers include *À double tour* (*Web of Passion*, 1959), *La Scandale* (*The Champagne Murders*, 1967) and *Le Boucher* (*The Butcher*, 1970); and Godard's *À bout de souffle* (*Breathless*, 1959) was a meditation on Bogart and the gangster film, his *Les Carabiniers* (1963) about the ideology of war and the war film. Both Godard and Truffaut ventured into science fiction, the former with *Alphaville* (1965) and the latter with *Farenheit 451* (1966).

Auteurism came to English-speaking film culture via the British magazine *Movie*, which began publication in 1962, and in the United States through Andrew Sarris, who in the early 1960s sought to provide auteurism with a theoretical foundation. Sarris posited what he called the auteur theory as three concentric circles – technical competence, distinguishable personality and interior meaning – and claimed that this vaguely defined interior meaning 'is extrapolated from the tension between a director's personality and his material' (1973: 51). Sarris does not explain this tension any further, but it may be understood, at least within the context of classic

Hollywood cinema, as the way a director mobilises, inflects or deploys the elements of genre he was obliged to use. Genre provides a frame within which auteurs can animate the elements of genre to their own purpose. Virtually all genre movies except those driven entirely by formula – those 'purist' genre movies dismissed by Robin Wood as existing in the 'simplest, most archetypal, most aesthetically deprived and intellectually contemptible form' (2003: 63) – reveal something of their maker.

The auteur approach caused considerable debate, in part due to the excessive claims made by its proponents. Chabrol, for example, argued that the less significant a film's narrative, the more room there is for the director to express his vision (1968: 77). Romantic and apolitical, auteurism again was attacked in the 1980s as film theory became more concerned with ideology, with the social, political and economic forces influencing both individual movies and cinema as an institution. In Peter Wollen's famous formulation (1972), critics were now interested in 'Howard Hawks' (a critical construct, signified by inverted commas) rather than Howard Hawks (the biological person). The director's name was no longer an artist but a concept that linked a series of film texts; no longer the source of the text but a reading strategy. Roland Barthes and others claimed that the author was dead, that he carried no authority over the meaning of the text, and that textual meaning thus could be appropriated by readers (1972: 142–8). Politically-oriented critical theory saw the author's personality as itself moulded by ideology and merely one of numerous codes shaping a given text. In France, in the wake of the events of May 1968, a new editorial board for *Cahiers du cinéma* grew more political and theoretical. Taking a position opposed to classic auteurism, they published a collectively written article on John Ford's *Young Mr. Lincoln*, a detailed analysis of the film showing how it was affected by studio politics, the Depression and cultural codes of representation, all of which are seen as influencing the film as much as the director's personal artistry.

In the end, the denial of the author as an embodied person was as excessive as earlier exaggerated assessments of greatness for many second-rank directors by zealous auteurists. Today critics, while acknowledging the collaborative nature of the filmmaking process, still discuss directors – and occasionally producers, screenwriters, cinematographers and actors – as auteurs, although such discussions are more grounded in historical, industrial and ideological contexts than in the past. The auteur approach has also been applied to other forms of popular culture, including television and popular music. Auteurism, although changed, has survived because, as Bruce Kawin points out, 'the special merit of the auteur theory is that it is capable of acknowledging the collaborative struc- ture of the cinematic enterprise *and* the evidence of patterns of coherence that have the integrity of authorship' (1987: 293).

Auteurism was less a theory than a concept for approaching a group of films and understanding relations between them – not unlike the idea of genre. Whatever its shortcomings, auteurism succeeded in turning critical attention from the content of films – Truffaut's tradition of quality – to their visual and formal qualities. Within the Hollywood context, this meant genre films. In the heyday of *Cahiers du cinéma*'s embrace of auteurism, André Bazin, editor of the journal, responded with his own article on 'La politique', concluding with the caution: 'Auteur, yes, but what of?' (1968: 155). As Bazin understood, auteur and genre are inextricable.

Case Study: John Ford and Stagecoach

John Ford made well over one hundred films in his long career, stretching from the silent era through to the 1960s, often dealing with periods and events in American history. In his work, this history is presented as a kind of pageant, like the imaginary cavalry riding by the window, representing the glory of national pride and tradition, at the end of his western *Fort Apache* (1948). Sarris describes Ford's films as possessing a 'double image', alter- nating 'between close-ups of emotional intensity and long shots of epic involvement, thus capturing both the twitches of life and the silhouette of legend' (1976: 85). This is particularly clear in *Stagecoach*, which frequently alternates between shots of individual passengers or groups of passengers on the stage and extreme long shots of the coach on its precarious journey through the wilderness. In *Stagecoach*, the long shots of the coach at the bottom of the frame moving through Monument Valley visually attests to civilisation's fragile toe-hold in the wilderness.

Peter Wollen declared his preference for Ford over Howard Hawks because, while Hawks' vision remained consistent throughout his very long career, Ford's evolved over time, making the thematic oppositions in his work more complex. Ford's vision of American democracy became increas- ingly disillusioned, not only giving his films a greater richness of theme, as Wollen argues, but also reflecting dramatic changes within American society. Before Ford was recognised as an auteur, his artistic reputation rested on his social problem films (*The Grapes of Wrath*) and aspiring art films (*The Informer*, 1935), but since the 1960s his westerns have attracted the most attention. For auteurists, Ford used the western and American history as a means of expressing his evolving regret for the nation's past.

The *Iron Horse* (1924) deals with the successful completion of the first continental rail line in 1869, a legendary moment in American history symbolising the triumph of civilisation over the wilderness. In *My Darling Clementine*, as already discussed, the celebration on the foundation of the unbuilt church in Tombstone is a lyrical evocation of the potential for true community. *Wagon Master* (1950), like *Stagecoach*, depicts a western journey in which an ideal democratic society is forged. In the same year as *Stagecoach*, Ford also made *Young Mr. Lincoln* and *Drums Along the Mohawk*. The former, although not a western, also shows this optimism in its depiction of the youthful Lincoln as a sagacious leader who in the final scene marches with determination into a gathering storm, metaphorical of the impending Civil War; the latter, a Revolutionary War western, ends with the raising of the new American flag, followed by a short montage of individual Americans in the fort looking at it with awe, including a burly smith (working man), black woman and even native American, who salutes it. The film's hero, Gil Martin (Henry Fonda, who also plays Lincoln in the other film) concludes *Drums Along the Mohawk* with a similarly portentous statement that they have 'a heap of work to do from now on'.

But Ford's post-war westerns are much darker. *The Searchers*, whose plot involves a lengthy search for a girl kidnapped by Apaches, exposes the racist ideology of the white civilisation that won the west. *Sergeant Rutledge* (1960), about a black cavalry officer court-martialled for rape and murder, shows the influence of the Civil Rights movement. Here, in contrast to Ford's earlier cavalry westerns from the 1940s such as *Fort Apache* and *She Wore a Yellow Ribbon* (1949) which depict the cavalry as a metaphor for a unified community, it is riven with racial tension. Ford's last western, *Cheyenne Autumn* (1964), presents the Indians as victims rather than villains, neglected by government bureaucracy on reservations and policed by an ineffective cavalry.

In Ford's last western, the elegiac *The Man Who Shot Liberty Valance* (1962), John Wayne plays western hero Tom Doniphon, the man who shoots the notorious outlaw Liberty Valance (Lee Marvin). Doniphon secretly shoots Valance from a dark alleyway when the lawyer Rance Stoddard (James Stewart), who knows nothing about guns, shows up for a shootout with the outlaw and fires his gun and misses. But after ridding the territory of evil, Doniphon then understands that he must step aside, literally into the shadows, giving way to the rule of law as represented by Stoddard, the attorney. Returning to the town years later, the now Senator Stoddard finds an unknown Doniphon about to be buried in a plain pine coffin without his boots, an ignominious end for the mythic cowboy hero. The film's main story is told in flashback, suffusing the action with a sense of time irretrievably past, as in film noir; and in the back room of the railway station an old stagecoach rests on blocks, gathering cobwebs, a relic from a bygone era.

Stagecoach, made at the height of Ford's optimism, achieves a fine balance of the genre's specific visual pleasures, the action and *mise-en-scène* audiences expect from a western, with generic innovation and authorial expressiveness. Frequently cited as the movie responsible for reviving interest in and the production of westerns, which was dominated by formula B-pictures and singing cowboy serials during the 1930s, *Stagecoach*'s story involves seven disparate passengers, along with the driver and a Marshall riding shotgun, on a perilous journey through the American southwest aboard a Concord stagecoach in the 1880s. The passengers include Mrs Mallory, an army officer's pregnant wife (Louise Platt); a southern gambler (John Carradine) who considers it his duty to protect her; Mr Peacock, a whiskey salesman (Donald Meek); an embezzling banker (Berton Churchill); and a prostitute (Claire Trevor) and drunken doctor (Thomas Mitchell) being driven out of town by self-appointed moral watchdogs. Along the way the stage picks up The Ringo Kid (John Wayne), who has just broken out of jail to avenge the deaths of his father and brother. The omnibus plot allows Ford, in the context of the western, to explore such themes as class and social prejudice, community and democracy. The fact that these otherwise very different characters, a cross-section of American types, are together in the first place is indicative of the democratic promise of the frontier.

The people on the stage travel on an epic journey through territory containing hostile Apaches, forcing the passengers to cooperate and show their mettle in order to arrive at their destination safely. Although the majestic panoramic shots of the stagecoach at the bottom of the frame, dwarfed by and moving through the magnificent mesas of Monument Valley, suggest the tenuous vulnerability of nascent civilisation in the wilderness, civilisation ultimately triumphs as the film imagines the establishment of a virtuous society among the microcosmic group. On the completion of the stagecoach's journey, the corrupt banker Gatewood is arrested, and class distinctions are erased as the southern gambler Hatfield is killed and both Mr Peacock and Mrs Mallory, who earlier had moved to the other end of the table, away from the prostitute Dallas, at Dry Fork, both acknowledge her as socially worthy.

Stagecoach relies heavily on genre conventions. Scenes such as the one in the saloon before the climactic showdown, with the piano player who stops playing with dramatic suddenness while the barkeep takes the mirror off the wall and stores it temporarily under the bar, are common to the western. The characters, too, are types familiar to the genre: the comic sidekick, the prostitute with the heart of gold, and so on. They fall neatly into pairs, making for a series of thematic contrasts that are variations of the genre's essential binary opposition between nature and culture, wilderness and civilisation, that is commonly seen as constituting the thematic

Figure 7 *Stagecoach*: Ringo and Dallas are the social outcasts

core of the western. So, for example, the timid whiskey salesman Peacock is, in some respects, the opposite of the pushy Gatewood, while the respectable officer's wife, Mrs Mallory, is contrasted with the fallen woman, Dallas. Dallas, in turn, is paired with Ringo in that they are both social outcasts because, as Dallas muses, 'things happen'. At the same time, Ringo's code of western justice is set against Hatfield's outmoded code of chivalry. Similarly, Gatewood and Doc Boone are both professional men, both fleeing from the clutches of Mrs Gatewood (Brenda Fowler), embodiment of some of those dubious 'blessings of civilisation' referred to by the Marshall at the film's end. But while the banker is socially respectable but inwardly corrupt and cowardly, the disgraced doctor is inwardly noble, like Dallas and Ringo, showing his true bravery during the Indian attack and later when he takes the shotgun away from Luke Plummer (Tom Tyler) before his showdown with Ringo.

Ford consistently uses the types and tropes of the western in *Stagecoach*, but provides them with depth and detail. For example, at one point on their journey when the trail is dusty, Hatfield offers Lucy Mallory a drink of water. The canteen is a familiar icon of the western, but Ford adds considerable complexity to the scene as Hatfield pours the drink for Mrs Mallory from the communal canteen into a silver cup which he takes from his breast pocket. The silver cup provides some important background information about Hatfield's aristocratic past and serves as a contrast to both the liquor bottles that Doc Boone swills from and to the more egalitarian western hero, Ringo. The latter follows by offering a drink to 'the other lady', Dallas, after Hatfield repockets the silver cup, an obvious social snub to her ('Sorry, no silver cups', says Ringo, with a guileless smile). The silver cup also functions as part of a network of water imagery across Ford's westerns, connecting *Stagecoach* with *3 Godfathers* (1948), in which water is crucial for the survival of the men and the baby left in their charge; *Fort Apache*, in which Captain Kirby York (John Wayne) praises the troopers as the ultimate embodiment of tradition and family because they would 'share the last drop in their canteens'; and *Cheyenne Autumn*, where the Indians stand stoically in the sun waiting for the representatives from Washington (who never arrive because of bureaucracy and politics), while water sits on a table nearby for the absent guests.

Similarly, when the baby is born in *Stagecoach*, all the men gather in hushed admiration in a tight circle, a brief but true community. Babies are important to Ford, part of the nuclear family which he cherishes and the promise of the future which is crucial for maintaining civilisation. Babies and children appear in numerous Ford films, perhaps most emphatically in *3 Godfathers*, in which the trio of bank robbers are spiritually reborn by their efforts to deliver a baby safely back to civilisation rather than escape arrest. In *Stagecoach* Ford emphasises the importance of the baby by inserting a cutaway of the helpless infant in Dallas' arms at the height of the dramatic Indian attack. The elitist characters ultimately accept Dallas because she helped with the delivery and subsequent caring of the baby for its weakened mother.

Ringo's quest for revenge, a common convention of the western, is never itself questioned, as it is in later psychological westerns like Fritz Lang's *Rancho Notorious* or Anthony Mann's *The Man From Laramie* (1955). According to Roland Barthes, as noted in the previous chapter, 'the very principle of myth' is that 'it transforms history into nature' (1972: 129). *Stagecoach* works in this manner in part by suggesting that Ringo's revenge quest is less a matter of personal than divine justice, a fated restoration of an overriding natural order (itself intimated in part by the contemplative grandeur of Monument Valley). In the end, *Stagecoach* asserts that there is no conflict between the moral individual and the demands of society, since moral authority will naturally transcend the legal. Curly, the Marshall, (George Bancroft) admits to the driver Buck (Andy Devine), that the territory definitely would be better off without the Plummers – a judgement that is shown to be entirely correct when we finally see Luke Plummer, a gruff, uncouth cowboy who guzzles his liquor, pushing dance hall girls around and intending to take a shotgun to the showdown.

Ringo departs at the end with Dallas, and with the blessing of Doc Boone and the Marshall, who bends the law when he lets Ringo go. In the end, Ringo rides out of town – but with a woman, not alone like Shane. A horseless cowboy at the beginning, now he rides a buckboard, western icon of the family and domesticity. As Doc Boone and Curly send Ringo and Dallas off, Doc says 'they're saved from the blessings of civilisation'. The line suggests perhaps that Ford's vision was already darkening in 1939, and the depiction of the ironically-named Lordsburg, with its saloons and brothels, supports such a view. Nevertheless, the film offers an apparent sense of closure in allowing Ringo and Dallas to escape from society and legal justice. The film also offered an upbeat message for pre-war America in which corporate evil is punished, heroic individual virtue triumphs and an ideal microcosmic democratic community is forged in the process. Even as Hitler was marching into European countries, *Stagecoach* imagined a cross-section of Americans who establish a classless, morally superior community forged by the crucible of the frontier, and who band together to defeat Geronimo, a 'butcher' who has 'jumped the reservation'.

Case Study: Howard Hawks and Red River

In its premiere issue in 1962, the British auteurist journal *Movie* provided a chart ranking directors, and only two were in the top ('Brilliant') category: Hitchcock and Hawks. Although hardly the memorable stylist that Hitchcock was (indeed, he once defined a good director as 'someone who doesn't annoy you'), Hawks was championed by auteurists because of his ability to work within so many genres and still express his distinctive concerns about professionalism. Hawks was a director who over the course of his long career liked to work within the given constraints of genre, and he forayed into most of the major genres in Hollywood cinema. Along with Frank Capra, he was the most important director of screwball comedies, a genre which he helped invent with *Twentieth Century* in 1934 and to which he contributed many of the best films, including *Bringing Up Baby* (1938) and *His Girl Friday* (1940). He also made detective noirs (*The Big Sleep*), gangster films (*Scarface*, 1932), adventure movies (*Hatari*, 1962), racing films (*The Crowd Roars*, 1932; *Red Line 7000*, 1965), war films (*Sergeant York*, 1941; *Air Force*, 1943), historical epics (*Land of the Pharaohs*, 1955), musicals (*Gentlemen Prefer Blondes*, 1953) and westerns (*Red River*; *Rio Bravo*; *The Big Sky*, 1952). This is precisely why, for Wollen, 'the test case for the auteur theory is provided by the work of Howard Hawks' (1972: 80).

Despite their generic heterogeneity, Hawks' films fall into two basic categories: adventure films and comedies. The adventure films tend to focus on stories of male professionals who are trying to accomplish a particular task or job. The male hero has a group of men gathered around him, also professionals who know how to work within the group to get the job done. The group is often removed in some way from society, and must work by its own rules. Frequently a woman appears who both threatens the professional cohesion of the group and with whom the hero has a romantic involvement. This pattern fits Hawks' movies as generically diverse as the adventure film *Only Angels Have Wings* (1939), the science fiction film *The Thing from Another World* (1951, credited to Christian Nyby but made by Hawks in all but name), and even a comedy like *Ball of Fire* (1941).

Crucial to appreciating Hawks as an auteur is Robin Wood's argument that Hawks' comedies are the flipside or inverse of the adventure films: that is, in the adventure movies, women typically represent emotional or sexual qualities that are distinctly non-professional, which Wood terms a 'lure of irresponsibility' that threatens to distract men from the job; in the comedies, however, these values are celebrated as a refreshing release or liberation from the demands of professionalism rather than a distraction from them. Wood cites the ending of *Bringing Up Baby* as an example of the comic inversion of professionalism. In the film, Dr David Huxley (Cary Grant), a palaeontologist who has spent years assembling a dinosaur skeleton, has had to endure a series of screwball adventures with socialite Susan Vance (Katherine Hepburn), whose dog has managed to take the skeleton's final bone and bury it somewhere on her rural Connecticut estate. Dr Huxley suffers a series of comically humiliating experiences engineered by Susan in order to regain possession of the bone. In the final scene he is back in the city at the museum, completing work on the assembled dinosaur skeleton atop a tall scaffolding when Susan enters and climbs up to him. When Huxley admits that he enjoyed their misadventures, the skeleton sways and collapses in a heap as he lifts her to the safety of the scaffolding. As Wood explains, 'the dry bones represent his life-work and are an image of his way of life, destroyed finally by the eruption of the Id' (1968: 71).

If professionalism suggests ossification and repression in the screwball comedies, in the adventure films getting the job done – whether it is defeating the alien in *The Thing*, defending the jail in *Rio Bravo*, or driving the cattle to market, as in the case of *Red River* – is paramount. Hawks' male groups have their own inner dynamics, and value and morality follow from accomplishing the task at hand by working as a team. In *The Thing*, when Captain Hendry's (Kenneth Tobey) crew discover the spaceship embedded in the ice, the men spread apart and with outstretched arms trace its shape and find they have formed a perfect circle: this fellowship of the ring is an essential Hawksian image in that it expresses at once the solidarity of the masculine group and male bonding, and its simultaneous exclusion of the Other, whether the feminine or alien 'super-carrot'.

Hawks' first western, *Red River*, also follows this pattern, but his vision ultimately conflicts with the requirements of the western, resulting in an unsatisfying tension between auteur and genre. The film tells the story of the first drive along the Chisholm Trail, a route used to drive cattle from Texas to Abilene, Kansas in the 1860s and through the 1870s. The film's sweeping narrative spans the initial settling of the west to the taming of the frontier and the development of a more complex post-Civil War market economy. As the film begins, Tom Dunson (John Wayne) leaves the wagon train with which he is heading west, and also his fiancée, to build his own cattle ranch on the Texas frontier in 1851. Shortly after his departure, the wagon train is attacked by Indians, and everyone is killed, except for a boy, Matthew Garth, whom Dunson and his friend Nadine Groot (Walter Brennan) find wandering in shock the next day. Dunson takes the land he wants from the Mexican aristocrat who currently owns it, and begins his herd. Fifteen years later, with the help of his now-grown adopted son Matt (Montgomery Clift), Dunson begins an unprecedented cattle drive north to Wichita. Dunson grows more tyrannical on the drive, threatening its success, eventually forcing Matt to intercede and take over. Against the wishes of Dunson, who is wounded in a gun battle with some deserting trail hands, Matt decides to gamble and drive the cattle to Abilene, hearing that the railroad has now reached this point further west. Dunson vows to kill Matt for what he regards as a betrayal. Matt completes the drive success-fully, falling in love with a woman, Tess Malloy (Joanne Dru), he meets in another wagon train along the way. Dunson rides into town seemingly determined to kill Matt, but in their climactic showdown, at the last minute he relents, the two men are reconciled and Matt receives Dunson's blessing to marry Tess.

In marked contrast to *Stagecoach*, with its embezzling banker, *Red River* is an unrepentant apology for capitalism. In the film the locomotive, icon of civilisation and industrialism on the frontier, is presented as unambiguously positive. The locomotive's billowing black smoke and deafening whistle do not despoil the landscape in *Red River* so much as boldly announce the triumphant advance of industry. Towns spring up along the railroad, allowing entrepreneurs like Dunson and Matt to get their product to market. The cattle buyer Melville (Harry Carey Sr), representative of the Greenwood Trading Company, is honest and straightforward, willing to pay top dollar for Matt's cattle because he has 'earned it', paralleling

Dunson's reasoning for adding Matt's name to the 'Red River D' brand at the end. The dramatic cattle drive may be understood as a microcosm for the American economy and capitalism, an interpretation made explicit in Dunson's impassioned speech about beef for the nation ('good beef for hungry people. Beef to make 'em strong, make 'em grow'). The beef for the nation in *Red River* also represents the new world order of rapidly expanding international markets for American goods – movies included – in a time when the nation was emerging as one of the world's two post-war superpowers.

From an auteurist perspective the cattle drive offers an archetypal Hawksian situation, as the men must take the cattle on an epic journey through a land of danger. Just as in *Stagecoach* the journey brings together a group of disparate individuals who forge a new democratic union, so in *Red River* a group of different men are brought together for the common purpose of the cattle drive. Unlike the group in *Stagecoach*, however, the group in *Red River* is all-male, an indication of the significant differences in the vision of the films' respective directors. While Ford and his male heroes appreciate the 'feminine' values of home and family, women have little place on Hawks' frontier, which is less a desert to be civilised than another space for testing masculine prowess, like the racetrack, the Andes or the Antarctic.

In *Red River* it is not Tess but Bunk Keneally (Ivan Parry), Groot's assistant cook, who provides this Hawksian group's encounter with the lure of irresponsibility. Tess is the ideal Hawksian woman, tough and knowing her place within the group. We first see her shooting during the Indian attack on the wagon train, but when Matt rides in, she quickly realises she is not as good a shot and promptly switches to loading. In *Red River*, rather than representing the threat to masculine professionalism as feminine, irresponsibility is depicted as immaturity, a metaphor Hawks would later literalise in *Monkey Business* (1952) in the form of a youth serum which causes people to regress mentally to childhood. In *Red River*, Bunk's childish sweet-tooth and his inability to control it causes a disastrous stampede when he tries to sneak one more fingerful of sugar and accidentally topples some pots and pans with a clatter, setting off the cattle and causing the death of one of the men. Dunson angrily accuses Bunk of 'stealing sugar like a kid' and wants to tie him to a wagon wheel for whipping (spanking).

Figure 8 *Red River*: the problem of male heroism

In the different responses of Dunson and Matt as group leaders to such problems, *Red River* explores what Wollen calls Hawks' major theme, 'the problem of heroism' (1972: 81). The film is full of typically Hawksian dialogue about professionalism, leadership and heroism, and the question of being 'good enough'. At the beginning of the film Dunson is the heroic pioneer, necessary for carving out the frontier, for helping in the establishment of civilisation. He leaves the wagon train, striking out on his own to begin his own herd. Someone must blaze the trail the wagon trains follow, and if anyone is capable of doing so it is the indomitable Dunson.

The wilderness in *Red River* lacks the sublime beauty of the Fordian frontier, with the iconic mittens and buttes of Monument Valley majestically thrusting skyward. Rather, Hawks' frontier in *Red River* is a harsh and contested space, one characterised by a social Darwinist struggle where only the fittest and fastest survive. When Dunson squares off against Don Diego's men, who immediately appear to challenge his claim to the land, there is no place to hide on the flat expanse of Texas plain. Only the most professional is good enough to take this land, to keep it, to use it to feed the nation. Dunson kills one of the men, and the next morning the first thing we see are buzzards circling overhead. Later, when the scene fades in after the passage of fifteen years, the elapsed time is indicated not only by Dunson's rising from a crouched position with the stiffness of age and discernibly greying temples, but also by the landscape, which is now marked by the graves of seven men who over the years had tried to take the land away from him.

With the passage of time, Dunson comes to seem more tyrannical than heroic. In a more civilised context, Dunson seems to grow increasingly tyrannical, declaring himself the law. On the drive, Teeler (Paul Fix) tells Dunson that he is crazy because 'this herd don't belong to you. It belongs to every poor hopin', prayin' cattleman in the whole wide state.' Wounded in the leg during the drive, Dunson becomes monomaniacal like Herman Melville's Ahab in *Moby Dick*, the obsessive one-legged captain who would also scuttle his command in his singular pursuit of vengeance. In obvious contrast to Dunson, Matthew Garth practises a more democratic form of leadership, thinking of the group rather than himself and leading them in a more consensual fashion.

The conflict between Dunson and Matt promises to reach its climax in a showdown, one of the western genre's most familiar conventions. But if generic logic requires the resolution of a shootout, Hawks' traditional notions of masculine professionalism supersede it. *Red River* obligingly foreshadows such a climax and hardily encourages viewers' expectation for it; yet in the end Hawks gives us reconciliation rather than confrontation. In fact, there are two anticipated showdowns in the film that fail to materialise. The first, between Matt and the hired gun Cherry (John Ireland), is foreshadowed by Dunson, who says they will 'paw at each other for a while' and then inevitably clash. But Matt and Cherry seem to have nothing but mutual respect for each other from the start, and Cherry even attempts (futilely) to defend Matt against Dunson. The second showdown, between Dunson and Matt, begins conventionally as Matt waits for Dunson on Main Street. But it collapses into horseplay between the two men until Tess intervenes, after which Dunson promises to add Matt's name to the brand and advises him to marry Tess. In the original story upon which the film is based, Dunson is fatally wounded by Cherry and then taken home to his ranch to die. At the end of *Red River*, though, the entire logic of the story, and the genre, is rejected to accommodate the happy ending that Hawks had said he wanted for what he once described as a 'love story between two men'.

From a Hawksian perspective, this narrative closure allows for the perpetuation of the male professional and the maintenance of masculine authority, a subtext exploited by the film's emphasis on guns as phallic power, particularly in the infamous scene where Matt and Cherry exchange and admire each other's pistols. Interestingly, no one in *Red River*, including Matt, disputes Dunson's right to ownership of the herd, or the necessity of Matt to 'earn' his initial on the 'Red River D' brand, even though the herd could not have existed without Matt's cow. Dunson may be a swaggering tyrant, but he is also a bold entrepreneur with a professional code, and as such Hawks is unable to let him die.

Case Study: Fritz Lang and Scarlet Street

Fritz Lang's work in film spans the silent era almost from its beginnings through the golden era of German Expressionism in the 1920s and the classic studio system in Hollywood to the rise of the international co-production. In the course of his career Lang directed more acknowledged classics of the German silent cinema than any other director, made the first important German sound film (*M*, 1932) and directed some of the most important crime films and film noirs of the American studio era, including *You Only Live Once* (1937), *Scarlet Street* (1945) and *The Big Heat* (1953). Critics have commonly divided Lang's extensive filmography into two major periods, the silent German films and the American studio movies. In the former he had considerable artistic freedom, while in Hollywood he worked against the greater constraints of the studio system, tight-fisted producers and B-picture budgets; yet the thematic and stylistic consistency in Lang's work across decades, countries and different production contexts is truly remarkable.

Lang's films consistently depict an entrapping, deterministic world in which the characters are controlled by both larger forces and internal desires beyond their understanding. In this cruelly indifferent world, people struggle vainly against fate and their own repressed inclinations toward violence. As in Hitchcock's films, Lang's often deal with the violent potential lurking within the respectable citizen and suggest that social order requires controlling the beast within. *M* is about a serial child killer

(Peter Lorre) who explains to the kangaroo court of criminals about to execute him that he is possessed by a murderous rage against which he is helpless. In *Fury* (1936), Lang's first American film, a barber tells his customer as he shaves him, razor poised at his neck, that 'people get funny impulses: if you resist them, you're sane; if you don't, you're on the way to the nuthouse, or the pen'. In *The Big Heat* good-hearted gangster's moll Debby Marsh (Gloria Grahame) is splashed in the face with boiling coffee – hideously scarred on one side but still beautiful on the other, her countenance an exteriorised expression of Lang's vision of the duality of human nature.

A more abstract, philosophical sense of an implacable fate also looms in Lang's films, as in *Der Müde Tod* (*Destiny*, 1921), where the hero tries to fight off Death. The Langian sense of fatalism comes largely through a *mise-en-scène* that is dark, geometrically rigid and that uses the frame as an enclosed space. Lang's work is so insistently enclosed that for Leo Braudy he is the auteur most fully representative of what he calls 'the closed style' of cinema, films in which 'the frame of the screen totally defines the world inside as a picture frame does' (1977: 48). The doom, paranoia and violence that suffuse Lang's vision was perfectly suited to the downbeat sensibility of film noir. The genre's dark vision of life is summed up by the detective (Dean Jagger) in *Dark City* (1950), who observes that 'people are like sheep frightened by the smell of death in a slaughterhouse: they run down the passageway with the other sheep, thinking there's freedom, but there's a man with a sledgehammer waiting'. Lang perfectly captures noir's merciless world near the end of *Scarlet Street*, when Johnny Prince (Dan Duryea), about to be executed in the electric chair for a murder he did not commit, screams 'gimme a break', only to be answered by the huge iron door of the execution chamber slamming shut, the camera watching dispassionately from a distance.

Scarlet Street tells the story of a loyal, meek company cashier and amateur painter, Christopher Cross (Edward G. Robinson), who meets a woman, Kitty March (Joan Bennett), on a deserted street late one evening, rescuing her from a man he thinks is an attacker but who is really her boyfriend Johnny Prince roughing her up. Kitty and Chris become involved, each lying to the other. Kitty exploits Chris for money, thinking he is a rich and famous artist, and Chris thinks she is a struggling actress who needs help getting her career started. Looking for an escape from his shrewish wife, Chris sets up Kitty with an apartment and comes there to paint. When he discovers the truth about Kitty, she mocks him, and in a fit of rage he grabs an ice pick and stabs her to death. Circumstantial evidence brings about the arrest, conviction and execution of Johnny, as Chris keeps silent. After the execution, Chris becomes tormented by a guilty conscience which haunts him with Kitty's taunting voice. As the film ends, he wanders the crowded city streets, a lonely, homeless and tormented bum.

Scarlet Street opens at a company party celebrating Chris's 25 years of service. Because of actor Robinson's strong iconographic association with the gangster film, we are encouraged to read the opening as a party scene out of a film like *Little Caesar* and to take Chris for a criminal. Robinson is shown in the centre of a long dinner table, smoking a cigar like his most famous character, Caesar Enrico Bandello. We quickly come to understand, however, that Chris is a timid, or rather repressed, law-abiding citizen. The deeper Langian irony is only revealed in retrospect, when Chris does indeed become a killer, revealing the criminal behind the common man. At the party, Chris sees his boss leave with an attractive younger woman who is obviously not his wife, and remarks that he would like to have a similar experience but never has. Shortly thereafter, on his way home through the city at night, which Lang presents as an expressionist mindscape – an elevated subway train flashes by, but generates no sound – Chris is presented with his secret desire. As if in a dream (lost, he tells a policeman he is 'all turned around'), suddenly there is Kitty, dressed in a transparent raincoat as if gift-wrapped, her charms clearly visible, being pushed around by Johnny Prince. Using his umbrella like a lance, Chris enacts the fantasy of a valiant knight coming to the rescue of a maiden in distress and apparently defeating the evil Prince, who flees the scene.

Repressed and emasculated, Chris works in an enclosed, partitioned office, where he doles out money to others. At home, his wife Adele (Rosalind Ivan) is a grotesque parody of a dominating shrew. Chris's horrible domestic life is underscored when Lang shows him in his apartment, the railing of the fire escape seeming like the bars of a prison cell while 'The Happy Household Hour' ironically broadcasts from a neighbour's radio off-screen. Chris paints to escape his bleak life, and enters into an affair with Kitty for the same reason (he describes painting to Kitty as being a 'love affair'). When Chris and Kitty meet for their first date in an outdoor restaurant, the camera cranes down from above the trees, where birds are singing, from the height of sunny optimism to show a more clouded view of relationships, as Chris and Kitty deceive each other about who they really are. As the camera descends, the song 'My Melancholy Baby' drops in register, and the romantic violins conventionally associated with romance give way to the more ominous cello on the soundtrack. The camera movement is like the opening of *Pennies from Heaven*, which shows a blue and sunny sky, but then the camera descends through a thick, dark, cloud layer into a grey world. In *Scarlet Street*, as in *Pennies from Heaven*, there are no blue skies, and a romantic vision is merely self-deception.

Chris Cross is aptly named, for the film shows this basically decent and mild-mannered man turning violent and vindictive, similar to the change that overtakes Vern (Arthur Kennedy) in Lang's western *Rancho Notorious* after his fiancée is raped and killed. At one point Johnny is shown hiding under a stairway, followed by a fade to a close-up of one of Chris's paintings depicting a city street with a huge snake wrapped around a pillar of the elevated subway. The snake appropriately occupies the same position within the frame where Johnny had been in the previous shot. Johnny also takes Chris's name, trying to collect on one of Chris's paintings that had been sold by a local art dealer. But it is Chris who becomes a contemptible snake toward the end of the film, criss-crossing with Johnny. After the murder, Chris hides beneath the stairs while Johnny comes in the building, in the same place Johnny had hidden earlier when Chris was coming to visit Kitty. As in the horror film, Johnny is like the return of the repressed for Chris.

Chris's paintings, as everyone observes, lack perspective, meaning that he does not see the depths of his own inner nature. They are described by the art critic David Janeway (Jess Barker) as having a 'masculine force', a quality that eventually proves to be true when Chris kills Kitty.

The ending of *Scarlet Street*, like the end of *Invasion of the Body Snatchers*, undermines narrative closure. The fact that Chris goes 'free' is not in itself as subversive as it may at first seem, since the Production Code specified that crimes not need necessarily be punished as long as the crime is depicted as wrong. Chris is trapped within his own guilt, just as one of the newspapermen covering Johnny's execution tells Chris all of us have a judge, jury and executioner inside us. Chris convicts himself mentally, and tries to execute himself by suicide, but is 'rescued' by well-intentioned neighbours who only preserve him for a prolonged agony.

Figure 9 *Scarlet Street*: violence lurks within the civilised man

More importantly, the ending does subvert one of the basic tenets of the Production Code, that the law of the land should not be shown as unjust. In convicting and executing Johnny, the law in *Scarlet Street is* responsible for a serious miscarriage of justice; on another level it is just, since it is Johnny who is responsible for creating and manipulating the situation and thus driving Chris beyond reason. Johnny is at least as guilty as Chris in Kitty's death even though he did not wield the knife. In the end, Lang has masterfully used the downbeat genre of film noir to explore his own recurrent theme of the nature of guilt and his vision of an implacable universe that refuses to give anyone a break.

Case Study: Melodrama, Douglas Sirk and All That Heaven Allows

Melodrama is a somewhat indistinct genre that refers to films about familial and domestic tensions. Originally the term, a hybrid deriving from a combination of music and drama, referred to stage plays that, beginning in the late eighteenth century, used music to emphasise dramatic or particularly emotional moments. More recently the category refers to narratives in any popular form that seem contrived or excessive in emotion and sentimentality, in which dramatic conflicts and plot take precedence over character and motivation, and in which there is a clear distinction between heroes and villains.

Melodrama tends to reduce history to the emotional problems of individual characters, as in historical melodramas like *Gone With the Wind* (1939) or *Kingdom of Heaven* (2005). Applying both psychoanalytic and Marxist theory to melodrama, Thomas Elsaesser has argued that the genre's frequently excessive style is symptomatic of the repressed emotions of the characters, who metaphorically embody the contradictions of bourgeois ideology that spill over into the *mise-en-scène*. The nuclear family, as in *All That Heaven Allows* (1955) and *Bigger Than Life* (1956), is frequently the site of these tensions. Feminist critics have been particularly interested in women's melodramas such as *Stella Dallas* (1925, 1937) and *Mildred Pierce* (1945), analysing how their representations of women are inscribed within domestic space and patriarchal ideology. These scholars are drawn to melodrama because it is the only genre (other than the musical) that regularly features female protagonists and is often narrated from their point of view.

Detlef Sierck first achieved success in post-World War One Germany in the theatre, directing the work of such classic playwrights as Ibsen, Shaw and Shakespeare. After a successful career at UFA, the dominant film studio in Germany after the rise to power of Hitler, Sierck came to Hollywood in 1937, one of many German émigrés to flee the Nazis. As Douglas Sirk, he made a number of competent studio pictures in the 1940s, but his greatest work was done a decade later. During his association with producers Albert Zugsmith and Ross Hunter at Universal-International studios beginning in 1951, he directed a series of melodramas including *All That Heaven Allows*, *Magnificent Obsession* (1954), *Written on the Wind* (1956), *A Time to Love and a Time to Die* (1958) and *Imitation of Life* (1959).

At one time Sirk was seen as a filmmaker who simply employed conventional Hollywood rhetoric, but his style is now regarded as a form of Brechtian distancing that draws the viewer's attention to the methods and purposes of Hollywood illusionism. Thus, rather than seeing his melodramas as mere reflections or endorsements of dominant ideology (category 'a'), they are read as deliberate, subtle critiques by a socially conscious artist who criticised Eisenhower's America from within mainstream filmmaking (category 'e'). Sirk's style hinges on a highly developed sense of irony, employing subtle parody, cliché and stylisation. The world of Sirk's melodramas is excessively lavish and patently artificial. The colours of walls, cars, costumes and flowers in his *mise-en-scène* are often harmonised in a constructed aesthetic unity markedly unlike the cacophony of colour in real life, but providing a comment on the oppressive, orderly world of the American middle class.

In *All That Heaven Allows* Carrie Scott (Jane Wyman) is a middle-aged widow who falls in love with her much younger gardener, Ron Kirby (Rock Hudson). The couple are truly in love and want to get married, but the people in Stoningham, the town where she lives, are (as the town's name suggests) cold and conventional suburbanites eager to cast the first stone by gossiping about her affair. Her children, Ned (William Reynolds) and Kay (Gloria Talbott), similarly disapprove of her relationship with Ron, wanting her instead to marry the elderly, more grandfatherly family friend Harvey (Conad Nagel), whom they praise as 'remarkably civilised'. Pressured on all sides, Carrie finally caves in and calls off the wedding. As time passes, Carrie suffers from headaches, and her doctor advises her to follow her heart rather than social decorum and return to Ron. Carrie goes to Ron's house in the country, but he is out hunting and as she drives away, Ron calls for her and in his eagerness falls off a snowy cliff. His injuries are serious but not fatal, and when she hears the news Carrie returns to Ron's place to care for him, now committed to stay with him.

The bourgeois world of *All That Heaven Allows* is an oppressive one that, as Barthes puts it, transforms nature into culture. Here it is not God's will but society that establishes moral sanctions, that determines whether Carrie's relationship is acceptable or not. This point is clearly established at the beginning of the film, as the camera first looks down from a height above the church steeple, and then cranes down into the street, where people are going about their lives. Later, when Kay tells her mother that her life would be ruined if Carrie were to marry Ron, light from a stained-glass window reminiscent of a church shines into the room.

Carrie's relationship becomes a site of ideological struggle, embodied in the film as an opposition between the narrow-minded townspeople and the more 'natural' Ron. Following Thoreau and his *Hamlet*-inspired dictum, Ron believes in the idea that 'to thine own self be true', while the townspeople all pretend to display social respectability. Sirk emphasises the difference between the two worlds by tending to depict the town in cool hues of blue and bold strokes of colour, while Ron and his space are associated with warm earthy shades of green and brown. A gardener, Ron lives in a greenhouse so that he can see the stars at night. His association with nature takes on connotations of sexual potency with the several references to his 'silver-tipped spruce'. Both worlds have parties, and are presented in stark contrast: the stiff and formal cocktail party at the country club, where Carrie brings Ron for a ritual of judgement and acceptance that ends disastrously, and the loose and spontaneous party of Ron and his friends, with its makeshift table and infectious good cheer.

Sirk is renowned for his thematic use of mirrors, shadows, glass and other elements of the *mise-en-scène* for dramatic and ironic purposes. In *All That Heaven Allows*, the scene of Carrie's children coming home to learn about her relationship with Ron begins with Carrie's face reflected in a small make-up mirror, mirroring the good face Carrie wants to project while the mirror's tight framing also foreshadows the children's negative response and the pressure they will put on her to end her affair. The guests at the cocktail party gather around the window, framing Ron and Carrie within their gaze as the couple will shortly be entrapped by their judgemental attitude. The gossip begins when busybody Mona (Jacqueline De Witt) spies Carrie going off with Ron; as she watches them from the butcher shop, Sirk adds a touch of irony by including the 'butcher' sign behind her.

A similar visual irony appears later, when Carrie's son Ned expresses his anger at her relationship. Carrie tells Ned that Ron should not come between them as the two speak in the living room where a room divider acts as a graphic wedge separating them within the frame. Her children's refusal to take Carrie's relationship with Ron seriously and their encouraging her instead to marry Harvey ultimately turns the family home into a trap. Kay tells Carrie about the ancient Egyptian practice of walling up widows with their dead husbands in their tombs; when she concludes by observing that she is glad such barbaric practices no longer happen, Carrie, whose late husband's ashes sit on the mantlepiece, asks wryly, 'Doesn't it?' When the children do not come home for Christmas, the camera looks through the window from the outside at Carrie on the inside looking out, sealed in alone during the holidays. As a Christmas gift, the children buy Carrie a television set. When the salesman delivers it, he says that on it you can see 'life's parade at your fingertips' as the camera dollies in so that the screen of the television set looms large in the image, with Carrie's face reflected in it. Carrie's children want her to live vicariously, through entertainment, but on that screen she can only see that life's parade will have passed her by.

All That Heaven Allows provides the kind of narrative closure characteristic of traditional genre films, but through irony and excess undermines it. Admiring the way Sirk was able to offer ideological critique within popular entertainment, German director Rainer Werner Fassbinder remade *All That Heaven Allows* as *Ali: Fear Eats the Soul* (1974), adding an element of race as well as age, while more recently Todd Haynes' *Far from Heaven* (2002) adds the further issue of homosexuality to the same story. In Sirk's film, as Carrie comes to the bedside of the concussed Ron, lying prone on the sofa, he wakes up and recognises her as she commits to being with him and nursing him. Just before Ron awakes, as if on a cue a deer trots into view through the picture window (a good description for mainstream film) behind them, a final connection between Ron and nature. Earlier, when Carrie and Ron first explore the old mill adjacent to the greenhouse and Carrie fantasises about living there with Ron, she sees an untended fireplace which she says if working would make the scene 'perfect'. In the final scene, along with the deer there is, of course, a blazing fire now in the hearth, making the scene in fact perfect. Yet Carrie doesn not really get what she wants, as she remains trapped in the role of caregiver. Sirk himself said that 'of course I had to go by the rules, avoid experiments, stick to family fare, have "happy endings", and so on' (quoted in Halliday 1971: 86). Rather than the denial of closure, as in *Invasion of the Body Snatchers* and *Scarlet Street*, *All That Heaven Allows* provides it so completely, so 'picture perfect', that it seems artificial and teeters on the edge of ringing hollow – a final ironic comment on the values of the society that, after all, is the audience for whom the film was made.

4 GENRE AND REPRESENTATION

Gender and Genre

Among their conventions, genre movies feature standard ways of representing gender, class, race and ethnicity. Into the 1980s, genres and genre movies remained almost exclusively the cultural property of a white male consciousness, the centre from which any difference regarding race, gender and sexuality was defined and marginalised. In all the action genres, it was white men who performed heroic deeds and drove the narrative. Movies such as *Westward the Women* (1951), in which a wagon train of women successfully makes the cross-country trek to California and the sexist trail boss (Robert Taylor) learns that some women also have what it takes to survive on the frontier, are only rare exceptions that prove the rule. In every type of action film, women and visible minorities assumed subsidiary and stereotyped roles, serving such narrative functions as helper or comic sidekick for the heroic white male.

The hypothetical viewer of Hollywood genre movies was traditionally, like almost all of the filmmakers who made the movies, white, male and heterosexual. This white masculine perspective was an inextricable part of the genre system, which was built upon certain gendered assumptions. Generally, the action genres – adventure, war, gangster, detective, horror, science fiction and, of course, the western – were addressed to a male audience, while musicals and romantic melodramas (also known as 'weepies') were marketed as 'women's films'. This distinction bespeaks wider patriarchal assumptions about gender difference in the real world.

As Molly Haskell rightly points out, 'What more damning comment on the relations between men and women in America than the very notion of something called the "woman's film"?' (1974: 153).

By the 1990s many genre movies attempted to open up genres to more progressive representations of race and gender, often deliberately acknowledging and giving voice to groups previously marginalised by mainstream cinema. In tune with contemporary notions of political correctness, films such as *The Adventures of Priscilla, Queen of the Desert* (1994), reconceived in Hollywood as *To Wong Foo Thanks for Everything, Julie Newmar* (1995), *The Doom Generation* (1995) and *Bound* (1996) pushed the boundaries of traditional generic representations. The film that provided the impetus for this new generic transformation was *Thelma & Louise* (1991), about two women who, finding themselves on the wrong side of the law, lead the police on a chase through the southwest. A big hit at the box office, *Thelma & Louise* is a generic hybrid of the western, the buddy film and the road movie – three of those genres traditionally regarded as male – and outlaw couple movies like *You Only Live Once*, *They Live by Night* (1949) and *Bonnie and Clyde* (1967). *Thelma & Louise* reversed Hollywood's conventional definition of woman's place as the domestic sphere and reimagined the buddy movie as female adventure. In the film's controversial ending, Thelma and Louise drive over the edge of the Grand Canyon rather than capitulate to the police. The last image is a freeze-frame of the car in mid-air, just beyond the apogee of its arching flight, followed by a fade to white.

This ending is, of course, a direct reference to one of the most famous of buddy movies, *Butch Cassidy and the Sundance Kid* (1969), and it sparked considerable debate regarding *Thelma & Louise*'s political value. Did it signify suicidal defeatism or triumphant transcendence? The contentious but popular reception of *Thelma & Louise*'s ending suggests how novel the film was at the time simply because of its gender substitution, since there had been no similar debate around the mythic ending of *Butch Cassidy and the Sundance Kid*. Regardless of how one reads the ending of *Thelma & Louise*, the fact that the film was the subject of such controversy suggests the difficulty of finding a place for women in action films and, more broadly, of gendered representations in popular cinema generally. After *Thelma & Louise*, many genre films seemed content merely to borrow its gender 'gimmick', simply plugging women and others into roles traditionally reserved for white men. But in reversing conventional representations, these films are prone to fall into the trap of repeating the same objectionable values. The question of whether female action heroes such as Sigourney Weaver's Ripley in *Alien* (1979) and its sequels, Linda Hamilton's Sarah Connor in *Terminator 2: Judgment Day* (1991), or the assassins played by Geena Davis in *The Long Kiss Goodnight* (1996), Uma Thurman in the *Kill Bill* films (2003, 2004) and the trio of actresses in the *Charlie's Angels* films (2000, 2003) are progressive, empowering representations of women or merely contained within a masculine sensibility has been a matter of considerable debate.

One film that successfully avoids this problem is Maggie Greenwald's western *The Ballad of Little Jo* (1993). The film is based on the true story of Josephine Monaghan, a woman who in the 1880s dropped out of New York society when she had a child out of wedlock, went west, and for the rest of her life passed as a man, making a successful career for herself as a sheep rancher in Idaho. Greenwald refuses to allow Little Jo, played by former model Suzy Amis, to become an object of the camera's traditionally male gaze as theorised by Laura Mulvey (1989). After escaping from her captors, Josephine obtains some men's clothes at a general store, and then, to the shock of the viewer, slashes her face with a knife from cheek to chin. Her scar becomes a badge of masculinity to the other men in the film, and it prevents the viewer from comfortably regarding her as an object of visual pleasure. As well, the film does not present much action in the form of gunplay – one of the appeals of the traditional western – but rather, emphasises domestic aspects such as homeopathic treatments and cooking.

The Ballad of Little Jo begins by showing a woman, Jo, in eastern dress incongruously walking down a road in the west, rather than the traditional cowboy hero riding into town. Men pass Josephine on horses, and one of them calls her a 'pretty filly'. A wagon loaded with goods appears in the foreground of the frame, momentarily blocking her from our view – just as men in effect negate her existence through oppression because of her gender. At last she is offered a ride by a passing peddlar, whom we subsequently discover has secretly sold her to some soldiers for their sexual pleasure. *The Ballad of Little Jo* begins, then, by using the imagery of the western to express the feminist insight that capitalism and patriarchy are intertwined, and that women are positioned as objects of exchange within that economy. Furthermore, by showing that gendered identity can be achieved by role playing and costume, the film foregrounds the post-modern idea of gender as performance rather than as immutable.

Case Study: Die Hard and the Action Film

Action and adventure films offer fast-paced narratives emphasising phys-ical action such as chases, fights, stunts, crashes and explosions, often dominating over dialogue and character development, as in movies like *Speed* and *The Rock* (1996). While action in film has been popular ever since the Lumières' train entered the station in one of the first films ever made (*L'Arrivée d'un train à La Ciotat*, 1895), the action film as a recognis-able genre for the definition and display of male power and prowess has its roots in the rousing swashbucklers of Douglas Fairbanks (*The Mark of Zorro*, 1920; *The Black Pirate*, 1922) and Errol Flynn (*Captain Blood*, 1935; *The Adventures of Robin Hood*, 1940). Since the blockbuster success of such movies as *Raiders of the Lost Ark* (1981) and its two sequels, the action film has developed into a distinct genre. In the 1970s and 1980s a number of innovative action films by directors such as John Carpenter and Walter Hill followed in the tradition of Howard Hawks, emulating that director's use of action and gesture as a physical index of professionalism. Carpenter's *Assault on Precinct 13* (1976), about a Los Angeles police station besieged by youth gangs, was based on Hawks' *Rio Bravo*, while his *The Thing* (1982) is a remake of the classic science fiction film of the same name produced by Hawks. Hill's *The Driver* (1978) and *Last Man Standing* (1996), a remake of the samurai film *Yojimbo* (1961), contain minimal dialogue, relying almost entirely on action to convey their narratives.

While earlier action heroes such as Victor Mature and Burt Lancaster were known for their broad, muscular physiques, since *Rocky* (1976) with Sylvester Stallone the criterion for action stars seems to be more on musculature than Method acting. Hypermasculine stars such as Stallone (*First Blood*, 1982; *Cliffhanger*, 1993), Jean-Claude Van Damme (*Kickboxer*, 1989; *Hard Target*, 1993), Steven Seagal (*Hard to Kill*, 1990; *Fire Down Below*, 1997), Chuck Norris (*Missing in Action*, 1984; *Invasion USA*, 1985) and Bruce Willis (the *Die Hard* series; *Last Man Standing*; *Hostage*, 2005), offer their impressive bodies for visual display and as the site of ordeals they must undergo in order to defeat the villains. Several critics have discussed the hyerbolic masculinity in these films as an expression of American ideology regarding politics and gender, reasserting male power and privilege during and after the Reagan administration (see, for instance, Tasker 1993; Jeffords 1994). The perfect embodiment of this excessive physicality is former bodybuilder Arnold Schwarzenegger, in such films as *The Running Man*, *Predator* (1987), *Total Recall* (1990) and of course, *The Terminator* (1984), in which he plays an emotionless killer robot. The essence of this new action hero is summed up in the scene in *Conan the Barbarian* (1982) in which Schwarzenegger, along with two dozen other slaves, is shown turning a giant gristmill; as the years go by the other men gradually disappear, leaving only Conan pushing the millstone himself.

Die Hard (1988) was one of the biggest box office hits of this action cycle, generating two sequels, *Die Hard 2* (1990) and *Die Hard with a Vengeance* (1995). The film's plot involves a tough New York cop, John McClane (Bruce Willis), who comes to Los Angeles for the first time to visit his estranged wife, Holly Gennaro (Bonnie Bedelia), in the office building where the company she works for is celebrating its Christmas party. McClane has hopes of convincing Holly to return to New York with him, but before they can fully discuss the matter a group of criminals pretending to be political terrorists take over the building, hold everyone at the party hostage and threaten to kill them in order to get a fortune in bonds stored in the company vault. Slipping away undetected and moving surreptitiously through the building, McClane manages single-handedly to outwit the savvy and ruthless leader, Hans Gruber (Alan Rickman), and kill all the members of the gang, as both the LAPD and FBI remain outside, unable to take action for fear of endangering the hostages. Once McClane saves the day, Holly reconciles with her husband.

The film shows its hero, like Conan, surviving multiple millstones and ultimately triumphing, but it is also explicit in linking the hero and his heroics to masculinity, patriarchy and their mythic representations. The narrative depicts a tough American male whose sense of masculinity is embattled: a working-class cop, he is uncomfortable in the lavishness of Nakatomi Tower and its white-collar world; more importantly, his wife has left him to pursue her own career and has retaken her maiden name. Ultimately, however, McClane gets to act as a rugged individual hero, and in the process of defeating the villains he reclaims both his masculine potency and his wife.

Figure 10 *Die Hard*: mythic male potency in the action film

The film depicts McClane's rugged individualism and heroic action largely through its generic references. For example, his name recalls *Big Jim McLain* (1952), starring John Wayne as a tough HUAC communist hunter in Hawaii. *Die Hard*'s plot overlaps with other action genres such as the heist film and the disaster film, and there are several references to McClane as a western hero. Like Shane, McClane rides into town (in a limousine rather than on a horse) at the beginning and rides out the same way at the end with Holly, like The Ringo Kid and Dallas at the end of *Stagecoach*. Not knowing McClane's real identity, Gruber sneeringly calls him 'Mr Cowboy'. When McClane falls into and then resurfaces from the artificial pond in the lobby of the office building during the climactic battle, he looks for a moment like Stallone as John Rambo in the jungles of Vietnam. (As the FBI approach Nakatomi Tower in a helicopter, one of them shouts: 'Just like fucking Saigon'.) Such generic references are particularly appropriate in a film like *Die Hard*, which works to restore the mythic potency to American masculinity.

In an era of Free Trade agreements, the film exploits a fear of foreign others as a threat to the American economy. Nakatomi Tower is a four-storey building that rises above other buildings in the area, a visual index of how the Japanese economic miracle has infiltrated to the point of dominating the American economy. The company president, Joseph Takagi (James Shigeta), is an Asian who has fulfilled the American Dream, rising to the top of a successful business. The leaders of the criminal gang are German and they often speak to each other in Hollywood pseudo-German, a caricature of villainy. The two main enemies of World War Two are like the return of the repressed in the horror film, their post-war economic success coming back to haunt America as the Japanese and the Germans compete to drain the country of its money, its economic potency.

In the scenario of action, Nakatomi Tower functions metaphorically as a big phallus, with muscular men vying for control and power. There are nude women in the nearest building and a pin-up of a female nude at the Tower's top. The Tower explodes in the film's climax, its orgiastic release of firepower followed by a coda in which McClane is reinstalled as head of his family, Holly resuming her married name. Appropriately, McClane saves Holly by stripping her of her Rolex, an icon of her success as a businesswoman: when he takes the watch off her wrist, Gruber, who had been clinging to it over the side of the Tower, falls to his death.

The movie is an action fantasy of the reinscription of the white American male as king of the hill. By the end, the evil Germans and industrious Japanese have been killed, and the African-American males seem clearly yet comfortably positioned as helpers: Sgt Al Powell (Reginald Veljohnson) takes his orders on the ground from McClane rather than his superiors, and Argyle (De'voreaux White) is his cheerful chauffeur. Gruber underestimates McClane as 'just another American who saw too many movies as a child. An orphan of a bankrupt culture who thinks he's John Wayne, Rambo, Marshall Dillon', but *Die Hard* references these and other action icons and films to reassert their masculine potency.

Case Study: Blue Steel

If *Die Hard* reveals how central masculinity is to the action film, then Kathryn Bigelow's films constitute a significant site of generic intervention. With *The Loveless* (co-directed with Monty Montgomery, 1983), *Near Dark* (1987), *Blue Steel* (1990), *Point Break* (1991), *Strange Days* (1995) and *K-19: The Widowmaker* (2002), Bigelow has established herself as the only female filmmaker thus far specialising in action films who can claim the status of auteur. Her action films employ a variety of stylistic means to question the masculinist values that drive action genres. They provide all the visceral thrills, the eroticised violence and physical action, the kinds of pleasures that viewers expect of action films; yet at the same time they also question the genre's traditional and shared ideological assumptions about gender, violence and spectatorship (see Jermyn & Redmond 2003; Grant 2004).

The action genre is perfectly suited to Bigelow's themes. The representation of violence is of course central to the genre, and as Steve Neale notes, the ideology of masculinity in popular cinema centres on 'notions and attitudes to do with aggression, power and control' (1993: 11). Bigelow's films explore the nature of masculinity and its relation to violence, especially within the context of spectatorship, often by playing on the gaze of the camera as conditioned by the generic expectations and conventions of traditional action films. Much as Sirk approached melodrama, providing their pleasures while critiquing the ideology that underpinned them, so Bigelow works within the action film, mobilising a range of the genres traditionally regarded as male precisely to interrogate the politics and pleasures of their gendered representations.

Blue Steel is about a rookie female cop, Megan Turner (Jamie Lee Curtis), whose gender troubles all the men in the film once she dons her uniform. Intervening in a supermarket robbery, Megan shoots and kills the holdup man, while one of the cowering bystanders in the store, Eugene Hunt (Ron Silver), secretly pockets the thief's handgun. As the film progresses, Eugene worms his way into Megan's life, at first romantically, but he grows increasingly psychotic, obsessed with the image of Megan wielding her weapon and usurping phallic power. Inevitably, there is a final violent confrontation between the two, and Megan manages to kill the seemingly unstoppable Eugene.

The violent struggle between them for control of the gun is not unlike the battle for the building in *Die Hard*, the gun in *Blue Steel* serving as the icon of masculine potency around which the action centres. From the opening credit sequence in which the camera magnifies the interior of a Smith and Wesson handgun, *Blue Steel* explores the action genre's iconographical fetishisation of the gun. Violence is associated with male animality in Bigelow's films because it is seen as an inherently masculine

Figure 11 *Blue Steel*: Megan usurps masculine power

quality. *Blue Steel* demonstrates this idea visually, emphasising the texture and tactile appeal of guns – the way hands caressingly grip them, how they slide across a table or are provocatively unbuttoned from a holster – as well as aurally, with careful Foley work on the soundtrack that magnifies the various sounds guns make.

Some critics have read *Blue Steel* as empowering for women, with Megan like the hero of a rape-revenge film, changing from being the victim of a stalker to defeating him. In this sense, the casting of Curtis (daughter of Janet Leigh, who played Marion Crane in *Psycho*) is particularly resonant, since she has been the tough 'final girl' (Clover 1992: 35ff) of several horror movies including the prototypical slasher film *Halloween* (1978), *Prom Night* (1980) and *Terror Train* (1980). It is Megan who defeats Eugene in battle, not her superior, the appositely named Detective Nick Mann (Clancy Brown). Another convention borrowed from the horror film is the doubling of Megan's abusive father (Philip Bosco) with Eugene, emphasising a continuity between apparently masculine norms and the horribly psychotic. The film employs other conventions of the horror film as well, particularly the werewolf film: Eugene is hirsute, with a dark beard, and associated with the night. At one point we see him digging for his gun like an animal under the full moon in New York's Central Park (his surname, tellingly, is 'Hunt').

Yet *Blue Steel* also suggests that the triumph of Megan and the femininity she represents can only be limited because of the entrenched power of patriarchy since the male world of Eugene is shown to be only a monstrous extension of normative masculinity. Eugene is a stockbroker, his position of economic privilege apparently allowing him the power to commit horrible criminal acts, including murder, with impunity. The film links Eugene's craziness to capitalism, competition, masculine identity and violence. No wonder Eugene hears voices in his head: on two occasions we see him screaming and wildly gesticulating in a sea of commodity traders, all male, on the floor of the stock exchange. It is in this same space that Eugene first fantasises shooting the gun he has picked up at the super-market. When Mann asks Megan why she became a cop, she ambiguously replies, 'Him', which, as Yvonne Tasker notes, may refer to her abusive father specifically or more generally to 'the man', to men, to the many potential Eugenes (1993: 161).

This association of masculinity with violence and animality appears throughout Bigelow's films: the hothead biker Davis (Robert Gordon) in *The Loveless* literally barks at his friends and yelps wildly as he fires his gun in the film's violent climax in the bar; in *Near Dark*, when Caleb (Adrian Pasdar) thinks he has killed the lead vampire by running him over with a semi truck, another icon of phallic power, he similarly howls with satisfaction. Megan's desire to be a cop thus becomes a desire to enter into the phallic domain, literalised in her struggle with Eugene over possession of the gun. Her uniform is a sign of transgression as Megan encroaches into a traditionally male world, an idea made clear early in the film in the montage of Megan suiting up for graduation. Individual shots fetishise parts of her uniform, reminiscent of the shots of the bikers' costumes in *The Loveless*. The character's gender is initially indeterminate, but then, as she buttons her shirt, we glimpse her lace bra underneath. Viewers are likely to be taken aback for a moment, 'disarmed' like the several men in the film when they see her in uniform for the first time or learn what her job is. Megan's wearing of a traditionally male uniform invokes genre conventions to suggest the extent to which those genres are shaped by the masculine propensity toward violence.

Race and Genre

Race, ethnicity and nationality are commonly stereotyped in genre films, sometimes together. African-Americans, as in *Die Hard*, have traditionally been cast in supporting roles, stereotyped as toms, coons, mulattoes, mammies and bucks (see Bogle 1973). Racial issues were addressed in a few special social problem films like *Home of the Brave* (1949), about black soldiers in the army, and *Pinky* (1949), about a light-skinned black woman passing as white (a theme also explored by Sirk in *Imitation of Life*). Since the 1990s, generic Arabs have been depicted in action movies as terrorists, as in *True Lies* (1994), *Executive Decision* (1996) and *The Siege* (1998). By contrast, Russians are friendlier in Hollywood movies following the collapse of the Soviet Union and the end of the Cold War, as in *The Hunt for Red October* (1990) and *Enemy at the Gates* (2001).

Asian-Americans have been largely absent from genre movies, as have Latinos until *West Side Story*. Outside Hollywood, there were separate but parallel Yiddish and black or 'race' cinemas. The 'golden age' of Yiddish film was the 1920s to the 1930s, black cinema from the 1930s to the 1940s. Both were institutionalised forms of cinema, with their own stars, directors, exhibition circuits and audiences. Both were organised along generic lines similar to Hollywood. There were, for example, black melodramas and musical westerns featuring African-American stars. Hollywood, too, tried all-black musicals such as *Hallelujah* (1929), *Cabin in the Sky* (1943) and *Carmen Jones* (1954), as well as dramatic films such as *Green Pastures* (1937) – the practice of segregating casts by race a reflection of the segregationist and discriminatory practices of the era in which they were made. Even in white Hollywood musicals, African-Americans tend to be separate from the narrative, whether it is Louis Armstrong in *Young Man with a Horn* (1950) and *High Society* (1956) or Chuck Berry in *Go, Johnny, Go* (1959) and *American Hot Wax* (1978). These performers appear as themselves, with a status that is in part 'outside' the story.

Except for such subsidiary and subordinate roles as maids, black faces were largely absent from Hollywood movies. Issues of race appeared, like the return of the repressed, safely coded within generic conventions, particularly in the western, which on the surface relegates the topic more safely to the nation's past rather than present. Since native Americans were victims of a genocidal policy of westward expansion, their image was easily appropriated for mythic use. This explains in part the convention of white men playing Indians in any roles more substantial than extras. The representation of the Indian as sexual threat can be seen in such films as D. W. Griffith's *The Battle of Elderbush Gulch* (1913) and John Ford's *Stagecoach*, both of which show well-intentioned men preparing to kill a young white woman to save them from 'a fate worse than death' – in other words, rape by the dark Other. The fear of miscegenation in the western is a convention that goes back to seventeenth-century captivity narratives, and conforms also with white fears about black sexuality. The success of *Broken Arrow* in 1950, with its liberal theme of racial tolerance between native Americans and whites, began a cycle of sympathetic Indian westerns such as *The Savage* (1952), *Seminole* (1953), *Apache* (1954) and *The Indian Fighter* (1955) that addressed issues of race somewhat more directly before the rise of the Civil Rights movement.

Other films, like *The Searchers* and *The Last Hunt* (1956), depict white racism rather than Indian brutality and sexual deprivation. *The Searchers* presents its protagonist, western icon John Wayne, as an overt racist. At the beginning of the film, Ethan Edwards (Wayne) returns to the Texas home of his brother Aaron several years after the end of the Civil War, having fought for the South and still wearing part of his Confederate uniform. His hatred of Indians is intense, as revealed by his scorn for Martin Pawley (Jeffrey Hunter), a half-breed, and by his defilement of Indian corpses, scalping them and shooting out the eyes of dead warriors so they cannot go to heaven. Soon after Ethan's arrival, Comanches lure Ethan away from the ranch and then kill Aaron and his wife Martha but take their two young daughters with them. Soon the younger girl is found dead, but Ethan and Martin spend years tracking down the older daughter, Debbie, although for different reasons: Martin wants to save Debbie not from the Comanche but from Ethan, who intends to kill her because he believes that miscegenation will pollute Debbie beyond redemption. When they find Debbie, they discover that she has become the 'wife' of a Comanche chief, Scar (Henry Brandon), and is apparently healthy and well. Ethan does have a change of heart at the last moment, sweeping Debbie into his arms to take her home as he is about to kill her; this ending, necessitated in part by the dictates of the star system and the importance of home and family for the director, hardly negates the virulent racism that characterises this western's hero throughout the entire film.

Encouraged by the success of *Cotton Comes to Harlem* in 1970, a cop film featuring two black detectives (Godfrey Cambridge and Raymond St. Jacques), a cycle of blaxploitation films followed. The term blaxploitation was coined by the trade paper *Variety* to describe these films, which appeared from the late 1960s through to the mid-1970s. Blaxploitation films are action films with sensationalist plots featuring stories of crime and violence in the inner city, with black actors in major roles and targeted specifically at black audiences.

As the Civil Rights movement gained momentum and became more militant, many black viewers rejected the more accommodating images of established black stars like Sidney Poitier and Harry Belafonte and welcomed the newer action movies with more macho black stars, such as ex-football Hall-of-Fame star Jim Brown in films like *Black Gunn* (1972) and *Slaughter* (1972). African-Americans responded to the change in representation 'from sambo to superspade' (Leab 1976), and Richard Roundtree became famous as the suave black detective John Shaft in *Shaft* (1971), billed as 'the new James Bond', as did Ron O'Neal as *Superfly* (1972). Pam Grier in *Coffy* (1973) and *Foxy Brown* (1974) and Tamara Dobson in *Cleopatra Jones* (1973) applied the same formula to female characters, creating 'supermacho females' (Guerrero 1993: 4).

Although some blaxploitation films were made by black filmmakers, many had white producers and directors and were made to cash in on the trend. Consequently, many of the black characters in these films are also stereotypes. The constraints of blaxploitation characterisation are parodied in Robert Townsend's *Hollywood Shuffle* (1987), a comedy about an aspiring black actor (played by the director) who goes to a black actors school where white instructors teach him how to talk jive and walk funky, and discovers that in Hollywood the only roles available to blacks are pimps, drug dealers or living-dead zombie pimps.

The formulaic nature of blaxploitation is also parodied in *Don't Be a Menace to South Central and Drink Your Juice in the Hood* (1996). The question of the extent to which blaxploitation was politically progressive has been a matter of debate, but the films did pave the way for a cycle of 'salt-and-pepper' (interracial) buddy movies beginning with *48 Hrs* (1982) and the wider acceptance of black action stars such as Wesley Snipes and Denzel Washington.

Case Study: Do the Right Thing

Do the Right Thing (1989), which brought a number of new African-American actors to the screen and started a cycle of black genre films in the 1990s, uses the conventions of many genres without fitting comfortably into any one. African-American filmmaker Spike Lee, director of *Do the Right Thing*, has tackled a number of genres, reworking them in a way that recalls Robert Altman's work in the 1970s. *School Daze* (1988) is a college musical, *Malcolm X* (1992) a biopic and *Get on the Bus* (1996) a road movie with a disparate group of black men who find themselves together on a chartered bus from L.A. to Washington to attend the Million Man March. *Bamboozled* (2000) is about the racist iconography and representation of popular culture. Its story of a new television show featuring deliberately retrograde representations of minstrels that becomes an unexpected hit is a variation of *The Producers* (1968) and examines the racist iconography of pop culture generally.

The story of *Do the Right Thing* takes place during one particularly hot summer day in the black neighbourhood of Bedford Stuyvesant in Brooklyn, New York and involves an ensemble of local characters. The action centres around Sal's Famous Pizzeria, where Mookie (Lee) works as a pizza delivery boy for Sal (Danny Aiello) and his two sons. Tensions begin to mount when Radio Raheem (Bill Nunn) and Buggin' Out (Giancarlo Esposito) ask for the pictures of some black brothers to be placed on the pizzeria's 'Wall of Fame', which is decorated with images of famous Italian-Americans like Frank Sinatra. Eventually tempers, like the temperature, rise to a boil, causing a racially-charged confrontation with police, who kill Radio Raheem and trigger a race riot. The film's graffiti-like style, with bold colour saturation, suggests the excessive look of melodrama – an appropriate approach given the overheated emotions of the characters.

The importance of such star iconography as displayed on Sal's 'Wall of Fame' informs the strategy of the entire film. As bold as its graffiti-like style, *Do the Right Thing* is filled with the iconography of black popular culture: Mookie's Jackie Robinson shirt, gerri curls, Mike Tyson, the casting of Ossie Davis and Ruby Dee (stars of the previous phase of integrationist black cinema), the loving litany of black jazz and R&B artists recited by the radio disc jockey Señor Love Daddy (Samuel L. Jackson), and so on. Accompanying the opening credits, the rap group Public Enemy attacks the

Figure 12 *Do the Right Thing*: the importance of iconography

white iconography of the entertainment industry by focusing on popular music in 'Fight the Power', its lyrics boasting that Elvis 'never meant shit to me'. Raheem and Buggin' Out's desire to place African-Americans on the white Wall of Fame is perhaps analogous to the position of Lee, making films with black content for black audiences within a system that is predominately white: wanting to get his films shown in theatres, he appropriates the iconography and conventions of classic Hollywood genre movies just as white popular culture had appropriated black styles in the past. This reappropriation is most explicit in the scene where Raheem repeats with a difference the famous monologue of conman Harry Powell (Robert Mitchum) posing as a minister in *Night of the Hunter* (1955), turning Mitchum's Southern drawl into urban street talk, and the discourse on love and hate from the metaphysical to the racial.

According to Henry Louis Gates Jr (1988) black literature is marked by a revision of, or a 'signifying' upon, texts in the Western (white) tradition. It is precisely in this play upon white texts, he argues, that black works articulate their difference. As the 'Night of the Hunter' scene makes manifest, *Do the Right Thing* signifies upon the conventions of dominant white cinema. For example, in the narrative there are no heroes, as in classic Hollywood cinema, only protagonists. All the characters are flawed in one way or another, and the film offers no comfortable site of spectator identification, as most Hollywood films tend to do. All of them talk to the camera, a convention of comedy, but here everyone hurls uncomfortable racial slurs at the viewer. *Do the Right Thing* also lacks closure, as nothing is resolved after the climactic riot, and none of the characters has an insight or revelation. There is no catharsis or satisfying denouement for viewers, and the film ends ambiguously by offering us two perspectives on the racial violence we have just seen: the peaceful integrationist message of Martin Luther King, and the more militant separatism of Malcolm X.

After *Do the Right Thing* a number of African-American directors emerged who, following Lee's lead, sought to penetrate mainstream cinema by signifying upon Hollywood iconography and genres. Robert Townsend's *The Five Heartbeats* (1991) is a backstage musical biopic about a fictional soul group, while his *The Meteor Man* (1993) is a science fiction film about a black man who attains astonishing powers from a meteor that lands in the 'hood. John Singleton's *Boyz n the Hood* (1991) is a crime film and a teen film, *Poetic Justice* (1993) a road movie starring Janet Jackson on a journey of self-discovery and *Higher Learning* (1995) a college movie, like *School Daze*. *Surviving the Game* (1994), by director and long-time Lee cinematographer Ernest Dickerson, inflects the classic thriller *The Most Dangerous Game* (1932) with the politics of race and class, as the human prey hunted for sport in this version are specifically poor urban blacks whom it is believed no one will miss. One distinct cycle that emerged during this period were 'hood films, also inspired by *Do the Right Thing*, such as *Boyz n the Hood, New Jack City* (1991), *Juice* (1992), *American Me* (1992) and *Menace II Society* (1993), that sought to capture the harsh realities of inner-city life by updating conventions of the classic gangster and crime film.

Case Study: Little Big Man and Posse

Before *Little Big Man* in 1970, director Arthur Penn had updated the western with a psychological study of Billy the Kid, *The Left-Handed Gun* (1958). Just as his *Bonnie and Clyde* offered a revision of the outlaw couple film for the counter-culture, so *Little Big Man* attempts to rewrite the western

Figure 13 *Little Big Man*: Custer's madness is a comment on traditional values

from the perspective of the native American. In the film, the Cheyenne refer to themselves as 'human beings', decentring the white point of view that dominates the western.

The story involves Jack Crabbe (Dustin Hoffman), a wizened man of almost 121 who claims to have fought with Indians during the Plains Wars and to be the sole survivor of the Battle of the Little Big Horn, Montana in 1876, where General George Armstrong Custer (Richard Mulligan) and his battalion of over 200 soldiers from the 7th Cavalry were killed by a combined force of Sioux and Cheyenne warriors. In the present, Jack tells his story to a historian (William Hickey), who is audio-taping the interview, and Crabbe's story is told in flashback. According to Crabbe, his family was killed during an attack on their wagon by a band of Cheyenne when he was a boy. Only he and his sister Caroline (Carole Androsky) survive, and she soon escapes, leaving young Jack to grow up as a Cheyenne brave. When he is caught during a skirmish between his Cheyenne band and some soldiers, he is returned to white civilisation, living in town with a stern minister (Thayer David) and his wife (Faye Dunaway). Over the course of the story, the appropriately named Jack Crabbe scuttles back and forth several times between white and Cheyenne society, always returning to the wise counsel of Old Lodge Skins (Chief Dan George), Jack's 'grandfather'. Along the way he becomes a gunfighter, earns his place as a Cheyenne brave, befriends Wild Bill Hickok (Jeff Corey) and tries to assassinate Custer.

With its narrative shuttling between white and Cheyenne society, *Little Big Man* is structured by a series of binary oppositions, points of contrast between the two worlds — not unlike the western itself, according to Jim Kitses. The native characters in the film are as fully developed as the white characters and as important within the narrative. Because Jack comes to one culture having become familiar with the other, we see white society from an Indian point of view and Cheyenne society from a white perspective. In *Stagecoach* and many traditional westerns, Indians emerge out of the landscape, with no apparent culture or purpose other than to threaten white civilisation. In *Red River*, when Groot sees the wagon train burning in the distance, he wonders 'why Indians always wanna be burning up good ... wagons for?' Most westerns avoid answering this question, but *Little Big Man* reveals the racist assumptions behind it.

Since the comparisons between the two cultures all favour Cheyenne society, the civilisation taken for granted in classic westerns is here consistently questioned. For example, the Cheyenne warrior Younger Bear (Cal Bellini), who hates Little Big Man for humiliating him by saving his life, nevertheless fulfills his duty by rescuing Little Big Man later, whereas a young white man sneaks up on Hickok and shoots him in the back for revenge. Regarding sexuality, Sunshine's (Amy Eccles) willingness to share her husband with her widowed sisters (in a scene of 'free love' with which the contemporary counter-culture audience might easily identify) and the Cheyenne's acceptance of the obviously gay Little Horse (Robert Little Star), who has chosen to live a domestic life rather than to hunt and fight with the other braves, is obviously preferable to the life of duplicity and repression that characterises Reverend Pendrake and his wife. Mr Merriweather (Martin Balsam), the snake-oil salesman, suggests that the universe is absurd, without meaning, and that as a result he is not any less moral than anyone else for being a charlatan, a confidence man. By contrast, the 'human beings', as they say, know where the centre of the earth is, and can accept the wholeness of life even if they cannot understand it ('sometimes the magic works and sometimes it doesn't', as Old Lodge Skins observes).

In reversing the depiction of Indians in relation to whites, the film also reverses other conventions and character types. For example, when the Cheyenne chase a stagecoach in *Little Big Man*, it is nothing more than a bulky conveyance that flops over unceremoniously, unlike Ford's mythic stagecoach that speeds on undeterred even when the driver is wounded, drops the reins and Ringo has to jump to the lead horses to regain them. Jack's sister Caroline, imagining herself the heroine of some captivity narrative, expects to be ravished by her Cheyenne captors, but she seems almost disappointed to find that they treat her respectfully. Also in *Little Big Man* the cavalry does not come to the rescue, as in *Stagecoach*, but rather brings death. The powerful scene of the Washita massacre, in which the cavalry rides in and lays waste to an Indian village, including women and children, could not help but invoke images of the Vietnam War, and especially the shocking revelations of the Mai Lai Massacre, for contemporary viewers in 1970 (the year of the film's release). The actress playing Jack's Cheyenne wife Sunshine looks as much Asian as she does native American. Aided by John Hammond's blues-tinged guitar and harmonica that provide the film's musical score, *Little Big Man* casts the Indians as victims of racial oppression.

Little Big Man acknowledges its own awareness of generic tradition and its attempt to rewrite it. When Jack enters what he calls his 'gunfighter phase', for example, he is dressed in an all-black costume reminiscent of that worn by countless movie cowboys. Generic elements are reversed or subverted in the film because it questions the myth of Manifest Destiny that the genre classically embraces. General Custer, as played by Richard Mulligan, is less the dapper but courageous military man played by the swashbuckling Erroll Flynn in *They Died with Their Boots On* (1941), made during World War Two, than an egomaniacal racist bordering on the psychotic. The stark difference between these two representations of a controversial military figure during two different war eras indicates the relative cultural consensus in the case of the former as compared to the strong division that characterised American society during the later conflict.

***

Although black cowboys did exist on the frontier, their history has been overwritten by the predominately white iconography of the western. One of the most popular genres of race films, as mentioned above, was the western, with the first possibly being *The Trooper of Troop K* (1917) with

Figure 14 *Posse*: a black western

black star Noble Johnson. In the late 1930s Herb Jeffries appeared in a series of independently produced all-black musical westerns including *The Bronze Buckaroo* (1939) and *Harlem Rides the Range* (1939). In 1960, Ford's *Sergeant Rutledge* starred Woody Strode as a cavalry soldier being court-marshalled because of his race. During the blaxploitation era several westerns were made, the most notable being *Buck and the Preacher* (1972), directed by Sidney Poitier, about white bounty hunters looking to return former slaves to work on southern plantations after the defeat of the South in the Civil War. Starring Harry Belafonte along with Poitier, *Buck and the Preacher* employed many conventions of the genre while foregrounding issues of race relations. But for the most part blacks had been absent from the Hollywood western – an absence so complete that it can serve as one of the major jokes in Mel Brooks's *Blazing Saddles*, which stars African-American actor Cleavon Little as a stylish 'Black Bart' with his Gucci designer saddlebags.

It is precisely this mythic erasure that Mario Van Peebles' *Posse* (1993) seeks to challenge. *Posse* opens with a black man speaking directly to the camera, presenting the entire story in flashback. This framing device refs back to *Little Big Man*, with its similar intent of revising western myth. Significantly, the interviewed witness in *Posse* is played by Woody Strode, himself an icon who had appeared in several of Ford's westerns. In a telling scene in *The Man Who Shot Liberty Valance*, Pompey (Strode), Tom Doniphon's hired hand, is sitting with the other students in a class on American history and democracy; when called upon to recite from 'The Declaration of Independence', looking downcast in a way that speaks volumes, he 'forgets' the part that says all men are created equal, after which he is brusquely ordered back to work by Doniphon. (Later Pompey is refused a drink in the saloon.) In Ford's films, Strode always embodied a respectful, subordinate presence; but in *Posse*, Strode expresses a more militant point of view, confronting the camera directly rather than averting his gaze, and criticising white people – that is, 'us', the normative spectators of the classic genre film – for having taken the land from native Americans.

As Strode tells the story, Jesse Lee (Van Peebles) and several other black soldiers (along with a 'token white', Jimmy Teeters (Stephen Baldwin)), desert from their company fighting in Cuba during the Spanish Civil War when they discover that their racist commander, Colonel Graham (Billy Zane), intends to kill them after they retrieve a fortune in gold that he plans to smuggle out of the country. Jesse Lee and the others manage to escape with the money to New Orleans, where they come into conflict with the law and have to flee west as outlaws. Out west, they go to Freemanville, an idyllic all-black community threatened by the Ku Klux Klan, pursued all the way by the vengeful Colonel Graham and his men. The film builds to a violent climax reminiscent of Peckinpah's *The Wild Bunch* as Jesse Lee encourages the townsfolk to take a stand against the white racists, and he also shoots it out with Graham and his men.

Posse uses many of the western's conventions and imagery reminiscent of western auteurs, but its most interesting aspect is the intrusion of contemporary elements into the narrative, creating a disjunction between setting and sensibility. This strategy is most apparent in the film's music, such as when the singer in the New Orleans brothel performs in a modern rhythm-and-blues style. Peckinpah once said that the western was a form with which it was possible to comment on society today, and that is Van Peebles' goal with the genre in *Posse*. The gang in *Posse* are a tight group of brothers who rise to the defence of their community, a message that also comes across in the urban 'hood films.

A title in *Posse*'s closing credits informs us that in fact one out of every three cowboys were black men, and that, 'although ignored by Hollywood and most history books, the memory of the more than 8,000 black cowboys that roamed the west lives on'. In *Liberty Valance*, the newspaper editor speaks for Ford when he says, 'When the legend becomes fact, print the legend.' *Posse*, by contrast, prefers to reclaim fact from the myth, reinserting blacks into western history, from which they have been largely written out in popular film.

CONCLUSION: BEYOND HOLLYWOOD

The Nation and National Cinema

A nation is a sovereign state that has its own government, borders, military and civil defence, as well as the symbolic iconography of nationhood such as flag, anthem and currency. Earlier conceptions of the nation-state were conceived primarily in essentialist terms, but more recent theoretical work on the idea of the nation and nationhood, as well as on national cinema, has problematised such monolithic claims. For Benedict Anderson (1983), a nation is an 'imagined community' which is understood as distinct and separate from all other nations by dint of the discourses it develops and the identity it creates for itself.

Today it is more difficult than even a century ago to define a nation. In the twentieth century vast waves of immigration, diasporas and disloca-tions of peoples occurred. National borders, like genres, are in process, despite attempts to preserve them. With the fall of the Soviet Union, new sovereign nation-states emerged and re-emerged in Eastern Europe. Also, there are nations without states, such as Palestine, and some states contain more than one nation, as in the case of the United Kingdom. In Canada, French-speaking Quebec is recognised by the rest of the country as a 'distinct society'. At the same time, we now live in a global village, with increasing numbers of people travelling more quickly and more frequently between countries and continents than in the past, and people are in constant communication around the world via the Internet and mobile telecommunications. Nevertheless, the idea of a nation is maintained by a wide variety of social and cultural institutions, ranging from literature and language to law and, of course, the media. The media allow for citizens to learn the news of the nation, to participate in its rituals and events and to rehearse the cultural myths of the nation through its popular culture.

Traditionally, the idea of national cinema has served as a category for the distribution and reception of non-Hollywood cinemas, as in the case of German expressionism and *Das Neue Kino* (New German Cinema), where the style or movement was in part manufactured as a way of distinguishing the nation's film product from Hollywood. In critical discourse, until recently, discussions of national cinemas have tended, as with genre, to identify distinctive narrative, visual and thematic patterns, and then read these patterns as somehow reflective of specific identifiable traits of the country's 'national character'. Again this idea has been challenged by the movement of filmmakers from one country to the next, not only on individual bases but also in the case of a large exodus, as when German directors, actors and craftspeople came to Hollywood from Nazi Germany in the 1930s. Furthermore, with international co-productions a common affair today, directors, actors and funding frequently come from multiple countries. For example, *Crouching Tiger, Hidden Dragon* (2000), which brought the Chinese swordplay movie to mainstream North American audiences, was funded by money from Taiwan, Hong Kong, the US and China.

Even the term 'Hollywood' itself is open to interrogation from the perspective of national cinema. Hollywood film is often equated with American cinema, but there are other filmmaking modes and practices that are outside Hollywood but part of American cinema, including experimental filmmaking, student and amateur filmmaking, documentary film and the well-established porn industry. In any case, the Hollywood studios are themselves owned by international media conglomerates. In 1985, for example, Twentieth Century Fox was purchased by Australian media baron Rupert Murdoch and became part of his News Corporation empire; in 1991 the Japanese Sony Corporation bought Columbia Pictures.

***

Although much theoretical work has been done to question hegemonic concepts of the nation, and hence of the idea of national cinema, the concept of genre is particularly useful for addressing the idea of national cinema generally as well as for conceptualising the contours of specific national cinemas. If a nation is an 'imagined community', it is also true Ella Shohat and Robert Stam point out (1996), that movie audiences are communities forged by spectatorship. Rick Altman describes such communities as 'constellated', by which he means a group of individuals who 'cohere only through repeated acts of imagination' – in the context of cinema, an imagined connection among geographically dispersed viewers who share similar spectatorial pleasures and generic knowledge (1999: 161–2). Genres, of course, would not be possible without such reading communities.

In developing a distinctive and vital national cinema, most countries have been forced to confront the global cultural domination of American film in some way. As Toby Miller observes, Hollywood is a global industry that sells its products in every nation around the world, with an international system of promotion and distribution. 'Hollywood', Miller notes, 'owns between 40 percent and 90 percent of the movies shown in most parts of the world' (2001: 3). At the level of government policy, many countries at one time or another have created quota regulations largely to combat the dominance of foreign – that is, essentially, American – films on domestic screens. But the American influence on other national cinemas exceeds mere numbers, for Hollywood – especially since the end of World War Two – has successfully dominated numerous foreign film markets on every continent, not only in terms of films shown and profits earned, but also, as *Kings of the Road* (*Im Lauf der Zeit*, 1976) directed by Wim Wenders (a German director who more than once has brilliantly used the American genre of the road movie) would have it, imaginations it has colonised. Even radical Third Cinema from Central and South America and Africa, in defining itself as 'imperfect' in opposition to First (Hollywood) and Second (European art film) Cinemas, has engaged in a dialectic with Hollywood.

Inevitably, as Tom O'Regan notes, national cinemas must 'carve a space locally and internationally for themselves in the face of the dominant international cinema, Hollywood' (1996: 5). Because Hollywood cinema is overwhelmingly a cinema of genre films, this means, in effect, working within the genre system, with its inherent constraints and possibilities. The frame of genre allows filmmakers the multiple benefits of working in forms familiar to audiences both at home and abroad, and thus offers more lucrative potential to producers for international distribution. Foreign distri-

FILM GENRE

bution is particularly important in countries where the population is insufficient to sustain an indigenous film industry, for it provides the only hope for films to return a profit. At the same time, however, accepting generic forms from Hollywood also threatens to overwhelm any distinctive national features that might be expressed in cinema. This dilemma has informed the discourse of national cinema in many countries, especially those which share English with Hollywood. In Australia, New Zealand, Great Britain and English-speaking Canada, dubbing or subtitling of prints is not required, making Hollywood films more accessible culturally and less expensive to distribute in these countries.

Filmmakers from around the world have responded to the domination of American film by adopting Hollywood genres and 'indigenising' or reworking them according to their own cultural sensibility (O'Regan 1996: 5), as in the case of the Italian 'spaghetti western', Hong Kong martial arts films and Mexican *la luche* films with superhero wrestlers like El Sante and the Blue Demon. British spiv films, French gangster movies, South Korean melodrama and Japanese *kaiju Eiga* (monster movies) all address specific national concerns even as they depend on their generic American predecessors for their meaning. The western, once the most familiar of movie genres worldwide, has spawned distinctive national takes in such films as *The Chant of Jimmie Blacksmith* (1978) and *The Proposition* (2005) from Australia, *Paperback Hero* (1973) and *The Grey Fox* (1982) from Canada, *El Topo* (*The Mole*, 1970) from Mexico and the Brazilian *Antonio das Mortas* (1969).

In some cases, filmmakers from elsewhere have demonstrated an ability to reinvigorate Hollywood genres with fresh ideas. In Germany, Fassbinder took the melodrama in more explicitly political directions in films such as *Ali: Fear Eats the Soul, Why Does Herr R Run Amok?* (1970; co-directed with Michael Fengler) and *Fox and His Friends* (1975), while John Woo (*The Killer*, 1989; *Hard Boiled*, 1992) in Hong Kong and George Miller (*Mad Max*, 1979; *The Road Warrior*, 1981; *Mad Max Beyond Thunderdome*, 1985) in Australia pumped a new kinetic energy into the action film. Often directors who exhibit a flair for genre filmmaking, like Woo, Miller and action stunt actor Jackie Chan, are lured to Hollywood and absorbed into the American film industry. With action films such as *Face/Off* (1997) and *Windtalkers* (2002), Woo has shown that it is possible for foreign directors who are auteurs to continue working in post-classical Hollywood.

Other filmmakers have mined popular genres while steadfastly remaining in their own countries. In New Zealand, Peter Jackson has succeeded in making genre movies that appeal to international (including American) audiences while at the same time inflecting them with issues of national culture and identity. *Bad Taste* (1987), Jackson's debut feature about a government team that combats aliens who have packaged the residents of a small village for their new intergalactic fast-food franchise, blends the iconography and conventions of horror (the proverbial old dark house, bodily violation), science fiction (aliens, space travel) and slapstick comedy. The film's most well-known moment, the accidental blowing up of a sheep with a bazooka, is an iconographic image that consciously bends horror convention to New Zealand content. Similarly, *Braindead* (1992) deftly synthesises comedy and splatter, using the violated bodies of the 'meat movie' as props for gags and situations that speak to national mythology.

Similarly, in Canada David Cronenberg has also worked in the horror genre, simultaneously appealing to American audiences while at the same time addressing Canadian cultural issues. In *Shivers* (1975), a mad scientist has invented a parasite that creates an insatiable sexual appetite in the host. The parasite escapes into a modern apartment building, Starliner Towers, spreading to the point that it becomes one large orgy. The film is a clever reversal of *Invasion of the Body Snatchers*, featuring zombie hosts to parasites that are sexually charged rather than affectless. In this scenario of uncontrolled free love, the so-called sexual revolution south of the border becomes the source of anarchy and horror, infiltrating the orderly world of Canadian society within the microcosm of the apartment building. The same fear animates *Videodrome* (1983), in which the body of a television producer is invaded by a hypnotic pirate television signal from somewhere in Pittsburgh containing addictive and mind-altering images of violence. Cronenberg's *mise-en-scène* in his horror films cleverly disguises Toronto to look like a generic American city, yet at the same time includes a few familiar landmarks for Canadian viewers to recognise and as a cue to read the films in terms of their cross-border cultural contexts.

Other national cinemas have also created their own genres. For example, German cinema in the 1920s and 1930s developed a distinctive genre of the mountain film, involving a character or group of characters striving to climb or conquer a mountain. The physical stamina and deter-mination required to scale mountains, as well as their monumentality and dwarfing of the individual (often shown in breathtaking location photog-raphy), seem to anticipate the fascist sensibility. Dr Arnold Franck, the most well-known director of mountain films, made Leni Riefenstahl a star in *Die Weiße Hölle vom Piz Palü* (*The White Hell of Pitz Palu*, 1929), and Riefenstahl directed her own mountain film, *Das Blaue Licht* (*The Blue Light*, 1932), before going on to make her infamous Nazi propaganda film *Triumph des Willens* (*Triumph of the Will*, 1936). The Heimatfilm, or 'Homeland film', is another German genre of sentimental, romanticised movies about rural Germany and its inhabitants. In Indian cinema, 'masala films' mix a variety of heterogenous generic elements, such as inserting musical sequences in a dramatic film, in a way uncharacteristic of Hollywood.

Samurai films, one of the period or costume (*jidai-geki*) genres in Japanese cinema that focuses on the figure of the samurai warrior, gained popularity in Japan after World War Two and became known in the West primarily through the films of Akira Kurosawa starring Toshiro Mifune, including *Yojimbo, Rashomon* (1950) and *Sanjuro* (1961). Focusing on the skills of the samurai, which rely on a strict code of discipline (*bushido*) not unlike the western hero's code of honour, the samurai film translated relatively easily into westerns. Several westerns have been remakes of samurai films: *The Outrage* (1964) was based on *Rashomon*; the spaghetti western *A Fistful of Dollars* (1964) and *Last Man Standing* were both based on *Yojimbo*. *Red Sun* (1971) paired Charles Bronson and Mifune in a buddy film in the American west, a formula more recently reiterated with Jackie Chan and Owen Wilson in *Shanghai Noon* (2000).

Audiences worldwide have been trained by the positioning and protocols of genre, and of Hollywood and classic narrative cinema more generally. Film noir, as both James Naremore (1998) and David Desser (2003) have demonstrated, has transcended the boundaries of a distinctly American film genre and become a global cultural phenomenon that far exceeds the US and even cinema itself. It is no surprise, then, that so many filmmakers outside of the US have made genre films. Already in the 1980s Alan Williams observed that '"genre" is not exclusively or even primarily a Hollywood phenomenon' and that 'we need to get out of the United States' (1984: 124). Nevertheless, while some work has been done in recent years on non-English genres such as Asian action films and melodrama, much more needs to be done. Many of these films remain largely unknown to Western audiences, but as the film industry and popular culture generally become increasingly globalised and populations become more multicultural, inevitably genres will interact more intensely across national boundaries.

FILMOGRAPHY

Abbott and Costello Meet Frankenstein (Charles Barton, 1948, US)
À bout de souffle (*Breathless*) (Jean-Luc Godard, 1959, France)
Àdouble tour (*Web of Passion*)(Claude Chabrol, 1959, France)
The Adventures of Priscilla, Queen of the Desert (Stephan Elliot, 1994, Australia)
The Adventures of Robin Hood (Michael Curtiz and William Keighley, 1938, US)
Air Force (Howard Hawks, 1943, US)
Alien (Ridley Scott, 1979, UK)
Alien Nation (Graham Barker, 1988, US)
Alien vs. Predator (Paul W. S. Anderson, 2004, US)
Ali: Fear Eats the Soul (Rainer Werner Fassbinder, 1974, Germany)
All That Heaven Allows (Douglas Sirk, 1955, US)
Alphaville (Jean-Luc Godard, 1965, France)
The Amazing Colossal Man (Bert I. Gordon, 1957, US)
American Hot Wax (Floyd Mutrux, 1978, US)
American Me (Edward James Olmos, 1992, US)
Andy Warhol's Dracula (*Blood for Dracula*) (Paul Morrissey and Antonio
     Margheriti, 1974, Italy/France)
Antonio das Mortas (Glauber Rocha, 1969, Brazil)
Apache (Robert Aldrich, 1954, US)
Apocalypse Now (Francis Ford Coppola, 1979, US)
Assault on Precinct 13 (John Carpenter, 1976, US)
Attack of the 50 Foot Woman (Nathan Juran, 1958, US)
Attack of the Puppet People (Bert I. Gordon, 1958, US)
Back to the Future III (Robert Zemeckis, 1990, US)
Bad Taste (Peter Jackson, 1987, New Zealand)
The Ballad of Little Jo (Maggie Greenwald, 1993, US)

Ball of Fire (Howard Hawks, 1941, US)
Bamboozled (Spike Lee, 2000, US)
The Band Wagon (Vincente Minnelli, 1953, US)
Battle Beyond the Stars (Jimmy T. Murakami, 1980, US)
The Battle of Elderbush Gulch (D. W. Griffith, 1913, US)
The Big Clock (John Farrow, 1948, US)
Bigger Than Life (Nicholas Ray, 1956, US)
The Big Heat (Fritz Lang, 1953, US)
The Big Sky (Howard Hawks, 1952, US)
The Big Sleep (Howard Hawks, 1946, US)
The Big Sleep (Michael Winner, 1978, UK)
Billy the Kid vs. Dracula (William Beaudine, 1966, US)
Black Gunn (Robert Hartford-Davis, 1972, US)
The Black Pirate (Albert Parker, 1926, US)
Blacula (William Crain, 1972, US)
Blade Runner (Ridley Scott, 1982, US)
Das Blaue Licht (*The Blue Light*) (Leni Rienfenstahl, 1932, Germany)
Blazing Saddles (Mel Brooks, 1974, US)
The Blob (Irwin S. Yeaworth Jr, 1958, US)
Blood Simple (Joel Coen, 1984, US)
The Blue Dahlia (George Marshall, 1946, US)
Blue Steel (Kathryn Bigelow, 1990, US)
Blue Velvet (David Lynch, 1986, US)
Body Heat (Lawrence Kasdan, 1981, US)
Bonnie and Clyde (Arthur Penn, 1967, US)
Le Boucher (*The Butcher*) Claude Chabrol, 1970, France)
Bound (Andy and Larry Wachowski, 1996, US)
Boyz n the Hood (John Singleton, 1991, US)
Braindead (Peter Jackson, 1992, New Zealand)
Brigadoon (Vincente Minnelli, 1954, US)
Bringing Up Baby (Howard Hawks, 1938, US)
Bring Me the Head of Alfredo Garcia (Sam Peckinpah, 1974, Mexico/US)
Broken Arrow (Delmer Daves, 1950, US)
Broken Arrow (John Woo, 1996, US)
The Bronze Buckaroo (Richard C. Kahn, 1939, US)
Brother Orchid (Lloyd Bacon, 1940, US)
Buck and the Preacher (Sidney Poitier, 1972, US)
Butch Cassidy and the Sundance Kid (George Roy Hill, 1969, US)
Captain Blood (Michael Curtiz, 1935, US)
Les Carabiniers (Jean-Luc Godard, 1963, France)

Carmen Jones (Otto Preminger, 1954, US)
The Chant of Jimmie Blacksmith (Fred Schepisi, 1978, Australia)
Charlie Chan Carries On (Hamilton MacFadden, 1931, US)
Charlie's Angels (McG, 2000, US/Germany)
Charlie's Angels: Full Throttle (McG, 2003, US)
Cheyenne Autumn (John Ford, 1964, US)
Chicago (Rob Marshall, 2002, US)
Chinatown (Roman Polanski, 1974, US)
Cliffhanger (Renny Harlin, 1993, Italy/France/US)
Coffy (Jack Hill, 1973, US)
Collateral (Michael Mann, 2004, US)
Conan the Barbarian (John Milius, 1982, US)
Coogan's Bluff (Don Siegel, 1968, US)
Cornered (Edward Dmytryk, 1945, US)
Cotton Comes to Harlem (Ossie Davis, 1970, US)
The Cowboys (Mark Rydell, 1972, US)
The Creature from the Black Lagoon (Jack Arnold, 1954, US)
Crocodile Dundee II (John Cornell, 1988, Australia/US)
Crouching Tiger, Hidden Dragon (Ang Lee, 2000, Taiwan/Hong Kong/US/China)
The Crowd Roars (Howard Hawks, 1932, US)
Dark City (William Dieterle, 1950, US),
Dark City (Alex Proyas, 1998, US)
Daughters of Darkness (Harry Kümel, 1971, Belgium/Italy/France/Germany)
Dawn of the Dead (George A. Romero, 1978, US)
Day of the Dead (George A. Romero, 1985, US)
Der Müde Tod (*Destiny*) (Fritz Lang, 1921, Germany)
Destry Rides Again (Benjamin Stoloff, 1932, US)
Destry Rides Again (George Marshall, 1939, US)
Detour (Edgar G. Ulmer, 1945, US)
Devil in a Blue Dress (Carl Franklin, 1995, US)
Die Hard (John McTiernan, 1988, US)
Die Hard 2 (Renny Harlin, 1990, US)
Die Hard with a Vengeance (John McTiernan, 1995, US)
Dirty Harry (Don Siegel, 1971, US)
Disraeli (Alfred E. Green, 1929, US)
DOA (Rudolph Maté, 1950, US)
DOA (Annabel Jankel and Rocky Morton, 1988, US)
Don't Be a Menace to South Central While Drinking Your Juice in the Hood (Paris
    Barclay, 1996, US)
The Doom Generation (Gregg Araki, 1995, US/France)

Do the Right Thing (Spike Lee, 1989, US)
Dracula (Tod Browning, 1931, US)
Dracula (John Badham, 1979, US)
The Driver (Walter Hill, 1978, US)
Drums Along the Mohawk (John Ford, 1939, US)
Duck Soup (Leo McCarey, 1933, US)
Easy Rider (Dennis Hopper, 1969, US)
Enemy at the Gates (Jean-Jacques Annaud, 2001, US/Germany/UK/Ireland)
Enemy Mine (Wolfgang Petersen, 1985, US)
Executive Decision (Stuart Baird, 1996, US)
Face/Off (John Woo, 1997, US)
Fantasia (Walt Disney, 1940, US)
Farenheit 451 (Francois Truffaut, 1966, UK)
Farewell, My Lovely (Dick Richards, 1975, UK)
Far from Heaven (Todd Haynes, 2002, France/US)
Fargo (Joel Coen, 1996, US)
Fatal Attraction (Adrian Lyne, 1987, US)
Fido (Andrew Currie, 2006, Canada)
Fire Down Below (Félix Enríquez Alcalá, 1997, US)
First Blood (Ted Kotcheff, 1982, US)
A Fistful of Dollars (Sergio Leone, 1964, West Germany/Spain/Italy)
The Five Heartbeats (Robert Townsend, 1991, US)
Follow the Fleet (Mark Sandrich, 1936, US)
Footlight Parade (Lloyd Bacon, 1933, US)
Force of Evil (Abraham Polonsky, 1948, US)
Fort Apache (John Ford, 1948, US)
48 Hrs. (Walter Hill, US, 1982)
42nd Street (Lloyd Bacon, 1933, US)
Foxy Brown (Jack Hill, 1974, US)
Frankenstein (James Whale, 1931, US)
Freddy vs. Jason (Ronny Yu, 2003, US)
The Gay Divorcee (Mark Sandrich, 1934, US)
Gentlemen Prefer Blondes (Howard Hawks, 1953, US)
Get on the Bus (Spike Lee, 1996, US)
The Girl Can't Help It (Frank Tashlin, 1956, US)
The Godfather (Francis Ford Coppola, 1972, US)
Gog (Herbert L. Strock, 1954, US)
Go, Johnny, Go! (Paul Landres, 1959, US)
Golddiggers of 1933 (Mervyn LeRoy, 1933, US)
Gone With the Wind (Victor Fleming, 1939, US)

Go West (Buster Keaton, 1925, US)
Go West (Edward Buzzell, 1940, US)
La Grande Illusion (Jean Renoir, 1937, France)
The Grapes of Wrath (John Ford, 1940, US)
The Great Train Robbery (Edwin S. Porter, 1903, US)
The Green Pastures (Marc Connelly and William Keighley, 1936, US)
The Grey Fox (Phillip Borsos, 1982, Canada)
The Gunfighter (Henry King, 1950, US)
Hallelujah (King Vidor, 1929, US)
Halloween (John Carpenter, 1978, US)
Hard-Boiled (John Woo, 1992, Hong Kong)
The Harder They Fall (Mark Robson, 1956, US)
Hard Target (John Woo, 1993, US)
Hard to Kill (Bruce Malmuth, 1990, US)
Harlem Rides the Range (Richard C. Kahn, 1939, US)
Hatari! (Howard Hawks, 1962, US)
Higher Learning (John Singleton, 1995, US)
High Noon (Fred Zinneman, 1952, US)
High Sierra (Raoul Walsh, 1941, US)
High Society (Charles Walters, 1956, US)
His Girl Friday (Howard Hawks, 1940, US)
Hollywood Shuffle (Robert Townsend, 1987, US)
Home of the Brave (Mark Robson, 1949, US)
Horror of Dracula (Terence Fisher, 1958, UK)
Hostage (Florent Emilio Siri, 2005, US/Germany)
House on 92nd Street (Henry Hathaway, 1945, US)
Hud (Martin Ritt, 1963, US)
The Hunt for Red October (John McTiernan, 1990, US)
The Hurricane (John Ford, 1937, US)
Im Lauf der Zeit (*Kings of the Road*) (Wim Wenders, 1976, Germany)
Imitation of Life (Douglas Sirk, 1959, US)
The Incredible Shrinking Man (Jack Arnold, 1957, US)
The Indian Fighter (André De Toth, 1955, US)
The Informer (John Ford, 1935, US)
Invasion of the Body Snatchers (Don Siegel, 1956, US)
Invasion U.S.A. (Joseph Zito, 1985, US)
The Iron Horse (John Ford, 1924, US)
It's Alive! (Larry Cohen, 1974, US)
It's Always Fair Weather (Stanley Donen and Gene Kelly, 1955, US)
It's a Wonderful Life (Frank Capra, 1946, US)

It, The Terror from Beyond Space (Edward L. Cahn, 1958, US)
I Walk Alone (Byron Haskin, 1948, US)
The Jazz Singer (Alan Crosland, 1927, US)
Juice (Ernest Dickerson, 1992, US)
Junior (Ivan Reitman, 1994, US)
K-19: The Widowmaker (Kathryn Bigelow, 2003, UK/Germany/US/Canada)
The Karate Kid (John G. Avildsen, 1984, US)
Kate and Leopold (James Mangold, 2001, US)
Key Largo (John Huston, 1948, US)
Kickboxer (Mark DiSalle and David Worth, 1989, US)
Kill Bill: Vol. 1 (Quentin Tarantino, 2003, US)
Kill Bill: Vol. 2 (Quentin Tarantino, 2004, US)
The Killer (John Woo, 1989, Hong Kong)
The Killers (Robert Siodmak, 1946, US)
Kindergarten Cop (Ivan Reitman, 1990, US)
Kiss of Death (Henry Hathaway, 1947, US)
Ladri di biciclette (*Bicycle Thieves*) (Vittorio de Sica, 1947, Italy)
Land of the Dead (George A. Romero, 2005)
Land of the Pharoahs (Howard Hawks, 1955, US)
The Last Hunt (Richard Brooks, 1956, US)
Last Man Standing (Walter Hill, 1996, US)
Last of the Mohicans (George B. Seitz, 1936, US)
Last of the Mohicans (Michael Mann, 1992, US)
The Last Seduction (John Dahl, 1994, US)
The Left-Handed Gun (Arthur Penn, 1958, US)
Little Big Man (Arthur Penn, 1970, US)
Little Caesar (Mervyn LeRoy, 1931, US)
Logan's Run (Michael Anderson, 1976, US)
Lonely are the Brave (David Miller, 1962, US)
The Long Goodbye (Robert Altman, 1973, US)
The Long Kiss Goodnight (Renny Harlin, 1996, US)
The Loveless (Kathryn Bigelow and Monty Montgomery, 1983, US)
M (Fritz Lang, 1932, Germany)
Mad Max (George Miller, 1979, Australia)
Mad Max: Beyond Thunderdome (George Miller, 1985, Australia)
Magnificent Obsession (Douglas Sirk, 1954, US)
The Magnificent Seven (John Sturges, 1960, US)
Malcolm X (Spike Lee, 1992, US)
The Maltese Falcon (John Huston, 1941, US)
The Man From Laramie (Anthony Mann, 1955, US)

The Man Who Shot Liberty Valance (John Ford, 1962, US)
The Man Who Wasn't There (Joel Coen, 2001, US)
Mark of the Vampire (Tod Browning, 1935, US)
The Mark of Zorro (Fred Niblo, 1920, US)
McCabe and Mrs. Miller (Robert Altman, 1971, US)
Mean Streets (Martin Scorsese, 1973, US)
Meet the Feebles (Peter Jackson, 1990, New Zealand)
Menace II Society (Albert and Allen Hughes, 1993, US)
The Meteor Man (Robert Townsend, 1993, US)
Mildred Pierce (Michael Curtiz, 1945, US)
Missing in Action (Joseph Zito, 1984, US)
Money Train (Joseph Ruben, 1995, US)
Monkey Business (Howard Hawks, 1952, US)
The Most Dangerous Game (Irving Pichel and Ernest B. Schoedsack, 1932, US)
Moulin Rouge! (Baz Luhrmann, 2001, US)
Murder, My Sweet (Edward Dmytryk, 1944, US)
My Darling Clementine (John Ford, 1946, US)
The Naked City (Jules Dassin, 1948, US)
Nashville (Robert Altman, 1975, US)
Near Dark (Kathryn Bigelow, 1987, US)
New Jack City (Mario Van Peebles, 1991, US)
New York, New York (Martin Scorsese, 1977, US)
Night of the Hunter (Charles Laughton, 1955, US)
Night of the Living Dead (George A. Romero, 1968, US)
Nosferatu (F. W. Murnau, 1922, Germany)
No Way Out (Roger Donaldson, 1987, US)
Obsession (Brian de Palma, 1976, US)
Once Upon a Time in the West (*C'era una volta il West*) (Sergio Leone, 1968, Italy)
Only Angels Have Wings (Howard Hawks, 1939, US)
On the Town (Stanley Donen and Gene Kelly, 1949, US)
Outland (Peter Hyams, 1981, UK)
Out of the Past (Jacques Tourneur, 1947, US)
The Outrage (Martin Ritt, 1964, US)
Paperback Hero (Peter Pearson, 1973, Canada)
Pat Garrett and Billy the Kid (Sam Peckinpah, 1973, US)
Le Peau Douce (François Truffaut, 1964, France)
Pennies from Heaven (Herbert Ross, 1981, US)
The Petrified Forest (Archie Mayo, 1936, US)
Phantom of the Paradise (Brian de Palma, 1975, US)
Pinky (Elia Kazan, 1949, US)

The Pirate (Vincente Minnelli, 1948, US)
Pitfall (André de Toth, 1948, US)
Poetic Justice (John Singleton, 1993, US)
Point Break (Kathryn Bigelow, 1991, US)
Posse (Mario Van Peebles, 1993, US)
The Postman Always Rings Twice (Tay Garnett, 1946, US)
The Postman Always Rings Twice (Bob Rafaelson, 1981, US)
Predator (John McTiernan, 1987, US)
The Proposition (John Hillcoat, 2005, Australia)
Psycho (Alfred Hitchcock, 1960, US)
Pursued (Raoul Walsh, 1947, US)
Raiders of the Lost Ark (Steven Spielberg, 1981, US)
Rancho Notorious (Fritz Lang, 1952, US)
Rashomon (Akira Kurosawa, 1950, Japan)
Red Line 7000 (Howard Hawks, 1965, US)
Red River (Howard Hawks, 1948, US)
Red Rock West (John Dahl, 1992, US)
Red Sun (Terence Young, 1971, Spain/Italy/France)
Ride the High Country (Sam Peckinpah, 1962, US)
Ride the Pink Horse (Robert Montgomery, 1947, US)
Rio Bravo (Howard Hawks, 1959, US)
The Road Warrior (George Miller, 1981, Australia)
The Rock (Michael Bay, 1996, US)
Rocky (John G. Avildsen, 1976, US)
Rosemary's Baby (Roman Polanski, 1968, US)
Rumble in the Bronx (*Hong Faan Kui*) (Stanley Tong, Hong Kong/Canada, 1996)
The Running Man (Paul Michael Glaser, 1987, US)
Sanjuro (Akira Kurosawa, 1961, Japan)
The Savage (George Marshall, 1952, US)
Le Scandale (*The Champagne Murders*) (Claude Chabrol, 1967, France)
Scarface (Howard Hawks, 1932, US)
The Scarlet Drop (John Ford, 1918, US)
Scarlet Street (Fritz Lang, 1945, US)
School Daze (Spike Lee, 1988, US)
Scream (Wes Craven, 1996, US)
The Searchers (John Ford, 1956, US)
Seminole (Budd Boetticher, 1953, US),
Sergeant Rutledge (John Ford, 1960, US)
Sergeant York (Howard Hawks, 1941, US)
Se7en (David Fincher, 1995, US)

Seven Brides for Seven Brothers (Stanley Donen, 1954, US)
The Seven Samurai (Akira Kurosawa, 1954, Japan)
Shaft (Gordon Parks, 1971, US)
Shanghai Noon (Tom Dey, 2000, US)
Shaun of the Dead (Edgar Wright, 2004, UK)
She Wore a Yellow Ribbon (John Ford, 1949, US)
Shivers (David Cronenberg, 1975, Canada)
The Shootist (Don Siegel, 1976, US)
The Siege (Ed Zwick, 1998, US)
Sisters (Brian de Palma, 1973, US)
Slaughter (Jack Starrett, 1972, US)
Somewhere in Time (Jeannot Szwarc, 1980, US)
Speed (Jan de Bont, 1994, US)
Stagecoach (John Ford, 1939, US)
Star Wars (George Lucas, 1977, US)
Stella Dallas (Henry King, 1925, US)
Stella Dallas (King Vidor, 1937, US)
Strange Days (Kathryn Bigelow, 1995, US)
Sunset Boulevard (Billy Wilder, 1950, US)
Superfly (Gordon Parks Jr, 1972, US)
Surviving the Game (Ernest Dickerson, 1994, US)
Swordfish (Dominic Sena, 2001, US)
T-Men (Anthony Mann, 1947, US)
The Terminator (James Cameron, 1984, US)
Terminator 2: Judgment Day (James Cameron, 1991, France/US)
Terror in a Texas Town (Joseph H. Lewis, 1958, US)
Thelma & Louise (Ridley Scott, 1991, US)
Them! (Gordon Douglas, 1954, US)
The Thing from Another World (Christian Nyby, 1951, US)
They Died with Their Boots On (Raoul Walsh, 1941, US)
They Drive by Night (Nicholas Ray, 1949, US)
They Live (John Carpenter, 1988, US)
3 Godfathers (John Ford, 1948, US)
THX-1138 (George Lucas, 1971, US)
A Time to Love and a Time to Die (Douglas Sirk, 1958, US)
Tirez sur le pianiste (*Shoot the Piano Player*) (François Truffaut, 1960, France)
To Wong Foo Thanks for Everything, Julie Newmar (Beeban Kidron, 1995, US)
El Topo (*The Mole*) (Alejandro Jodorowsky, 1970, Mexico)
Total Recall (Paul Verhoeven, 1990, US)
Touch of Evil (Orson Welles, 1958, US)

Triumph des Willens (*Triumph of the Will*) (Leni Rienfenstahl, 1936, Germany)
A Trooper of Troop K (Harry A. Gant, 1917, US)
True Lies (James Cameron, 1994, US)
Twentieth Century (Howard Hawks, 1934, US)
Two Mules for Sister Sarah (Don Siegel, 1970, US)
Vampire in Brooklyn (Wes Craven, 1995, US)
Van Helsing (Stephen Sommers, 2004, US/Czech Republic)
The Velvet Vampire (Stephanie Rothman, 1971, US)
Videodrome (David Cronenberg, 1983, Canada)
The Virginian (Victor Fleming, 1929, US)
The Virginian (Stuart Gilmore, 1946, US)
Wagon Master (John Ford, 1950, US)
The Warriors (Walter Hill, 1979, US)
Watermelon Man (Melvin Van Peebles, 1970, US)
Die Weiße Hölle vom Piz Palü (*The White Hell of Pitz Palu*) (Arnold Franck and Georg Wilhelm Pabst, 1929, Germany)
West Side Story (Robert Wise, 1961, US)
Westward the Women (William A. Wellman, 1951, US)
White Zombie (Victor Halperin, 1932, US)
Who Framed Roger Rabbit (Robert Zemeckis, 1988, US)
The Wild Bunch (Sam Peckinpah, 1969, US)
Windtalkers (John Woo, 2002, US)
Written on the Wind (Douglas Sirk, 1956, US)
Yojimbo (*The Bodyguard*) (Akira Kurosawa, 1961, Japan)
Young Frankenstein (Mel Brooks, 1974, US)
Young Man with a Horn (Michael Curtiz, 1950, US)
Young Mr. Lincoln (John Ford, 1939, US)
You Only Live Once (Fritz Lang, 1937, US)

BIBLIOGRAPHY

The bibliography lists works cited in the text and is also designed to point to useful further reading. The annotated list of 'essential reading' highlights works considered to be of particular importance to contemporary understandings of film genre, although many valuable contributions are also to be found under 'secondary reading' and in volumes on individual genres.

ESSENTIAL READING

Altman, Rick (1999) *Film/Genre*. London: British Film Institute.
  Accessible and wide-ranging discussion on genre theory, criticism and development.
Barthes, Roland (1972) *Mythologies*. Ed. and trans. Annette Lavers. New York: Hill and Wang.
  Pioneering semiological analyses of ideology within the artifacts of popular culture.
Bordwell, David, Janet Staiger and Kristin Thompson (1985) *The Classic Hollywood Cinema: Film Style and Mode of Production to 1960*. New York: Columbia University Press.
  Exhaustive study that analyses the style of typical Hollywood movies and the function of the studio system.
Cawelti, John (1985) *The Six-Gun Mystique*. Bowling Green, OH: Popular Press.
  Major study of the western genre and popular art across several forms and media of popular culture, including cinema.
Frye, Northrop (1970) *Anatomy of Criticism: Four Essays*. New York: Atheneum.
  Foundational genre study of formulas and modes in literature.
Grant, Barry Keith (ed.) (2003) *Film Genre Reader 3*. Austin: University of Texas

Press.
Central collection of important essays on genre theory and individual genres.
Neale, Steve (1980) *Genre*. London: British Film Institute.
Brief but important early work of film genre theory.
____ (2000) *Genre and Hollywood*. New York and London: Routledge. *Ambitious examination of the studio system and a number of genres including the critical debates they have engendered.*
Schatz, Thomas (1981) *Hollywood Genres: Formulas, Filmmaking and the Studio System*. New York: Random House.
Important study of the Hollywood genre system and six major genres.
Wollen, Peter (1972) *Signs and Meaning in the Cinema*, revised edn. Bloomington and London: Indiana University Press.
Influential work of film theory with relevant chapters on the auteur theory and semiology of the cinema.

SECONDARY READING

Adorno, Theodor W. and Max Horkheimer (1997) 'The Culture Industry: Enlightenment as Mass Deception', in *Dialectic of Enlightenment*. New York and London: Verso, 120–67.
Alloway, Lawrence (1971) *Violent America: The Movies 1946–1964*. New York: Museum of Modern Art.
Altman, Rick (ed.) (1980) *Genre: The Musical*. London: Routledge and Kegan Paul.
____ (1987) *The American Film Musical*. Bloomington: Indiana University Press.
Anderson, Benedict (1983) *Imagined Communities*. London: Verso.
Aquila, Richard (ed.) (1996) *Wanted Dead or Alive: The American West in Popular Culture*. Urbana and Chicago: University of Illinois Press.
Aristotle (1982) *Poetics*. Trans. James Hutton. New York: Norton.
Arnold, Matthew (1960 [1882]) *Culture and Anarchy*. London and New York: Cambridge University Press.
Bazin, André (1968) 'La Politique des Auteurs', in Peter Graham (ed.) *The New Wave*. New York: Doubleday/London: British Film Institute, 137–55.
____ (1971a) 'The Evolution of the Western', in *What is Cinema?*, vol. II. Ed. and trans. Hugh Gray. Berkeley: University of California Press, 149–57.
____ (1971b) 'The Western, or the American Film *par excellence*', in *What is Cinema?*, vol. II. Ed. and trans. Hugh Gray. Berkeley: University of California Press, 140–8.
Bogle, Donald (1973) *Toms, Coons, Mulattoes, Mammies, and Bucks*. New York: Viking.
Borde, Raymond and Etienne Chaumeton (2002) *A Panorama of American Film*

Noir. Trans. Paul Hammond. San Francisco: City Lights.

Bordwell, David (1979) 'The Art Cinema as a Mode of Film Practice', *Film Criticism* 4, 1, 56–64.

Bourget, Jean-Loup (2003 [1973]) 'Social Implications in the Hollywood Genres', in Barry Keith Grant (ed.) *Film Genre Reader 3*. Austin: University of Texas Press, 51–9.

Braudy, Leo (1977) *The World in a Frame: What We See in Films*. Garden City, NY: Anchor Doubleday.

Brooks, Van Wyck (1970 [1915]) *Three Essays on America*. New York: Dutton.

Browne, Nick (ed.) (1988) *Refiguring American Film Genres: History and Theory*. Berkeley: University of California Press.

Buscombe, Ed (ed.) (1990) *The BFI Companion to the Western*. New York: Atheneum.

_____ (2003 [1970]) 'The Idea of Genre in American Cinema', in Barry Keith Grant (ed.) *Film Genre Reader 3*. Austin: University of Texas Press, 12–26.

Caughie, John (ed.) (1981) *Theories of Authorship*. London: Routledge & Kegan Paul.

Cavell, Stanley (1981) *Pursuits of Happiness: The Hollywood Comedy of Remarriage*. Cambridge: Harvard University Press.

Cawelti, John (1976) *Adventure, Mystery, and Romance: Formula Stories as Art and Popular Culture*. Chicago: University of Chicago Press.

_____ (1985) *The Six-Gun Mystique*. Bowling Green, OH: Popular Press.

_____ (2003 [1979]) '*Chinatown* and Generic Transformation in Recent American Films', in Barry Keith Grant (ed.) *Film Genre Reader 3*. Austin: University of Texas Press, 243–61.

Chabrol, Claude (1968) 'Little Themes', in Peter Graham (ed.) *The New Wave*. New York: Doubleday/London: British Film Institute, 73–7.

Clover, Carol J. (1992) *Men, Women and Chainsaws: Gender in the Modern Horror Film*. Princeton, NJ: Princeton University Press.

Cohan, Steven and Ina Rae Hark (eds) (1993) *Screening the Male: Exploring Masculinities in Hollywood Cinema*. London and New York: Routledge.

Collins, Jim (1992) 'Genericity in the Nineties: Eclectic Irony and the New Sincerity', in Jim Collins, Hilary Radner and Ava Preacher Collins (eds) *Film Theory Goes to the Movies*. New York and London: Routledge, 242–63.

Collins, Richard (1970) 'Genre: A Reply to Ed Buscombe', *Screen*, 11, 4–5 (August–September), 66–75.

Comolli, Jean and Jean Narboni (1977 [1969] 'Cinema/Ideology/Criticism (1), *Screen Reader*, London: SEFT, 2–11.

Cook, Pam (1976) 'Exploitation Films and Feminism', *Screen*, 17, 2 (Summer), 122–7.

Cook, Pam and Mieke Bernink (eds) (1999) *The Cinema Book*, 2nd edn. London: British Film Institute.

Creed, Barbara (1993) *The Monstrous-Feminine: Film, Feminism, Psychoanalysis*. London: Routledge.

Damico, James (1978) 'Film Noir: A Modest Proposal', *Film Reader* 3, 48–57.

Desser, David (2003) 'Global Noir: Genre Film in the Age of Transnationalism', in Barry Keith Grant (ed.) *Film Genre Reader 3*. Austin: University of Texas Press, 516–36.

Dixon, Wheeler Winston (ed.) (2000) *Film Genre 2000*. Albany: State University of New York Press.

Doane, Mary Ann (1987) *The Desire to Desire: The Woman's Film of the 1940s*. Bloomington and Indianapolis: Indiana University Press.

Doherty, Thomas (1988) *Teenagers and Teenpics: The Juvenilization of American Movies in the 1950s*. Boston: Unwin Hyman.

Douglas, Drake (1969) *Horror!* New York: Macmillan.

Durgnat, Raymond (1967) *Films and Feelings*. Cambridge, MA: MIT Press.

Eisenstein, Sergei (1949 [1936]) 'Through Theatre to Cinema', in Jay Leyda (ed.) *Film Form: Essays in Film Theory*. New York: Harcourt, Brace & World, 3–17.

Elsaesser, Thomas (2003 [1973]) 'Tales of Sound and Fury': Observations on the Family Melodrama', in Barry Keith Grant (ed.), *Film Genre Reader 3*. Austin: University of Texas Press, 363–95.

Feuer, Jane (1982) *The Hollywood Musical*. Bloomington: Indiana University Press.

Focillon, Henri (1942) *Life of Forms in Art*. New York: George Wittenborn.

Forster, E. M. (1927) *Aspects of the Novel*. New York: Harcourt, Brace & World.

Frayling, Christopher (1981) *Spaghetti Westerns*. London: Routledge & Kegan Paul.

Gallagher, Tag (2003 [1986]) 'Shoot-Out at the Genre Corral: Problems in the "Evolution" of the Western', in Barry Keith Grant (ed.) *Film Genre Reader 3*. Austin: University of Texas Press, 262–76.

Gates, Henry Louis Jr (1988) *The Signifying Monkey: A Theory of Afro-American Literary Criticism*. New York: Oxford University Press.

Gehring, Wes D. (ed.) (1988) *Handbook of American Film Genres*. New York: Greenwood Press.

Gledhill, Christine (ed.) (1987) *Home Is Where the Heart Is: Studies in Melodrama and the Woman's Film*. London: British Film Institute.

Graham, Peter (ed.) (1968) *The New Wave*. Garden City, NY: Doubleday.

Grant, Barry Keith (1986) 'The Classic Hollywood Musical and the "Problem" of Rock 'n' Roll', *Journal of Popular Film and Television*, 13, 4 (Winter), 195–205.

____ (ed.) (1996) *The Dread of Difference: Gender and the Horror Film*. Austin:

University of Texas Press, 1996.

_____ (ed.) (2003) *John Ford's Stagecoach*. Cambridge and New York: Cambridge University Press, 2003.

_____ (2004) 'Man's Favourite Sport?: The Action Films of Kathryn Bigelow', in Yvonne Tasker (ed.) *Action and Adventure Cinema*. London and New York: Routledge, 371–84.

Grant, Barry Keith and Christopher Sharrett (eds) (2004) *Planks of Reason: Essays on the Horror Film*, 2nd edn. Lanham, MD: Scarecrow Press.

Guerrero, Ed (1993) *Framing Blackness: The African-American Image in Film*. Philadelphia: Temple University Press.

Halliday, Jon (1971) *Sirk on Sirk*. London: Secker & Warburg/British Film Institute.

Harris, Kenneth Marc (1990) 'American Film Genres and Non-American Films: A Case Study of *Utu*', *Cinema Journal*, 29, 2 (Winter), 36–59.

Haskell, Molly (1974) *From Reverence to Rape: The Treatment of Women in the Movies*. Baltimore: Penguin.

Hutchings, Peter (1995) 'Genre Theory and Criticism', in Joanne Hollows and Mark Jancovich (eds) *Approaches to Popular Film*. Manchester and New York: Manchester University Press, 59–77.

Jeffords, Susan (1994) *Hardbodies: Hollywood Masculinity in the Reagan Era*. New Brunswick, NJ: Rutgers University Press.

Jenkins, Henry (1993) *What Made Pistachio Nuts?: Early Sound Comedy and the Vaudeville Aesthetic*. New York: Columbia University Press.

Jermyn, Deborah and Sean Redmond (eds) (2003) *The Cinema of Kathryn Bigelow: Hollywood Transgressor*. London: Wallflower Press.

Kaminsky, Stuart M. (1974) *American Film Genres: Approaches to a Critical Theory of Popular Film*. Dayton, OH: Pflaum.

Kaplan, E. Ann (ed.) (1980) *Women in Film Noir*, revised edn. London: British Film Institute.

Kawin, Bruce (1987) *How Movies Work*. New York: Macmillan/London: Collier-Macmillan.

Keane, Stephen (2006) *Disaster Movies: The Cinema of Catastrophe*, second edition. London: Wallflower Press.

King, Geoff (2002) *Film Comedy*. London: Wallflower Press.

King, Geoff and Tanya Krzywinska (2000) *Science Fiction Cinema: From Outerspace to Cyberspace*. London and New York: Wallflower Press.

Kitses, Jim (1970) *Horizons West*. Bloomington: Indiana University Press/London: British Film Institute.

Klinger, Barbara (2003 [1986]) '"Cinema/Ideology/Criticism" Revisited: The Progressive Genre', in Barry Keith Grant (ed.) *Film Genre Reader 3*. Austin: University of Texas Press, 75–91.

Knight, Arthur (2002) *Disintegrating the Musical: Black Performance and American Musical Film*. Durham, NC: Duke University Press.

Krutnik, Frank (1991) *In a Lonely Street: Film Noir, Genre, and Masculinity*. London and New York: Routledge.

Landy, Marcia (ed.) (1991) *Imitations of Life*. Detroit: Wayne State University Press.

Leab, Daniel J. (1976) *From Sambo to Superspade: The Black Experience in Motion Pictures*. Boston: Houghton Mifflin.

Leitch, Thomas (2002) *Crime Films*. Cambridge and New York: Cambridge University Press.

Lévi-Strauss, Claude (1977) *Structural Anthropology*. Harmondsworth, Middlesex: Penguin.

MacDonald, Dwight (1964 [1953]) 'A Theory of Mass Culture', in Bernard Rosenberg and David Manning White (eds) *Mass Culture: The Popular Arts in America*. New York: Free Press/London: Collier-Macmillan, 59–73

Mast, Gerald (ed.) (1982) *The Movies in Our Midst*. Chicago and London: University of Chicago Press.

____ (1987) *Can't Help Singin': The American Musical on Stage and Screen*. New York: Overlook Press.

McArthur, Colin (1972) *Underworld USA*. New York: Viking Press/London: British Film Institute.

McCarthy, Charles and Todd Flynn (eds) (1975) *Kings of the Bs: Working within the Hollywood System*. New York: Dutton.

McDonald, Paul (2000) *The Star System: Hollywood's Production of Popular Identities*. London: Wallflower Press.

McHugh, Kathleen and Nancy Abelman (2005) *South Korean Golden Age Melodrama: Gender, Genre, and National Cinema*. Detroit: Wayne State University Press.

Mercer, John and Martin Shingler (2004) *Melodrama: Genre, Style, Sensibility*. London: Wallflower Press.

Miller, Toby, Nitin Givil, John McMurria and Richard Maxwell (2001) *Global Hollywood*. London: British Film Institute.

Motion Picture Producers and Distributors of America (1982) 'The Motion Picture Production Code of 1930', in Gerald Mast (ed.) *The Movies in Our Midst*. Chicago: University of Chicago Press, 321–32.

Mulvey, Laura (1989) *Visual and Other Pleasures*. Bloomington and Indianapolis: Indiana University Press.

Naremore, James (1998) *More Than Night: Film Noir in its Contexts*. Berkeley and Los Angeles: University of California Press.

Neale, Steve (1993 [1983]) 'Masculinity as Spectacle: Reflections on Men and

Mainstream Cinema' in Steven Cohan and Ina Rae Hark (eds) *Screening the Male: Exploring Masculinities in Hollywood Cinema*. London and New York: Routledge, 9–20.

_____ (ed.) (2002) *Genre and Contemporary Hollywood*. London: British Film Institute.

_____ (2003 [1990]) 'Questions of Genre', in Barry Keith Grant (ed.) *Film Genre Reader 3*. Austin: University of Texas Press, 164–97.

Neale, Steve and Murray Smith (eds) (1998) *Contemporary Hollywood Cinema*. London and New York: Routledge.

Nowell-Smith, Geoffrey (1968) *Visconti*. Garden City, NY: Doubleday.

O'Regan, Tom (1996) *Australian National Cinema*. London and New York: Routledge.

Powdermarket, Hortense (1950) *Hollywood: The Dream Factory*. Boston: Little, Brown.

Propp, Vladimir (1968 [1927]) *Morphology of the Folk Tale*. Trans. Laurence Scott. Austin and London: University of Texas Press.

Pye, Douglas (2003 [1975]) 'The Western (Genre and Movies)', in Barry Keith Grant (ed.) *Film Genre Reader 3*. Austin: University of Texas Press, 203–18.

Ray, Robert B. (1989) *A Certain Tendency of the Hollywood Cinema, 1930–1980*. Princeton, NJ: Princeton University Press.

Redmond, Sean (ed.) (2004) *Liquid Metal: The Science Fiction Film Reader*. London: Wallflower Press.

Rubin, Martin (1999) *Thrillers*. New York and Cambridge: Cambridge University Press.

Ryall, Tom (1970) 'The Notion of Genre', *Screen*, 11, 2 (March–April), 22–32.

_____ (1998a) 'British Cinema and Genre', *Journal of Popular British Cinema*, 1, 18–24.

_____ (1998b) 'Genre and Hollywood', in John Hill and Pamela Church Gibson (eds) *The Oxford Guide to Film Studies*. Oxford and New York: Oxford University Press, 327–37.

Ryan, Michael and Douglas Kellner (1988) *Camera Politica: The Politics and Ideology of Contemporary Hollywood Film*. Bloomington and Indianapolis: Indiana University Press.

Sargeant, Jack and Stephanie Watson (eds) (1999) *Lost Highways: An Illustrated History of Road Movies*. London: Creation Books.

Sarris, Andrew (1973) 'Notes on the Auteur Theory in 1962', in *The Primal Screen*. New York: Simon and Schuster, 38–53.

_____ (1976) *The John Ford Movie Mystery*. London: Secker & Warburg/British Film Institute.

_____ (1985) *The American Cinema: Directors and Directions 1929–1968*. Chicago:

University of Chicago Press.

Saunders, John (2001) *The Western Genre: From Lordsburg to Big Whiskey.* London: Wallflower Press.

Schaefer, Eric (1999) *'Bold! Daring! Shocking! True!': A History of Exploitation Films, 1919–1959.* Durham and London: Duke University Press.

Schrader, Paul (2003 [1972]) 'Notes on Film Noir', in Barry Keith Grant (ed.) *Film Genre Reader 3.* Austin: University of Texas Press, 229–42.

Shadoian, Jack (1977) *Dreams and Dead Ends: The American Gangster/Crime Film.* Cambridge, MA: MIT Press.

Shohat, Ella and Robert Stam (1996) 'From the Imperial Family to the Transnational Imaginary: Media Spectatorship in the Age of Globalization', in Robin Wilson and Wimal Dissanayake (eds) *Global/Local: Cultural Production and the Transnational Imaginary.* Durham: Duke University Press, 47–92.

Silver, Alain and James Ursini (1996) (eds) *Film Noir Reader.* New York: Limelight.

Slotkin, Richard (1992) *Gunfighter Nation: The Myth of the Frontier in Twentieth-Century America.* New York: Atheneum.

Sobchack, Thomas (2003 [1975]) 'Genre Film: A Classical Experience', in Barry Keith Grant (ed.) *Film Genre Reader 3.* Austin: University of Texas Press, 103–14.

Sobchack, Vivian (1980) *The Limits of Infinity: The American Science Fiction Film.* New York: A. S. Barnes.

Sontag, Susan (1966) *Against Interpretation and Other Essays.* New York: Delta.

Staiger, Janet (2003 [1997]) 'Hybrid or Inbred: The Purity Hypothesis and Hollywood Genre History', in Barry Keith Grant (ed.) *Film Genre Reader 3.* Austin: University of Texas Press, 185–99.

Tasker, Yvonne (1993) *Spectacular Bodies: Gender, Genre and the Action Cinema.* London and New York: Routledge.

_____ (ed.) (2004) *Action and Adventure Cinema.* New York and London: Routledge.

Telotte, J. P. (ed.) (1991) *The Cult Film Experience: Beyond All Reason.* Austin: University of Texas Press.

_____ (2001) *Science Fiction Film.* New York: Cambridge University Press.

Tudor, Andrew (1973) *Theories of Film.* New York: Viking Press/London: British Film Institute.

Turner, Graeme (1993) 'The Genres are American: Australian Narrative, Australian Film, and the Problems of Genre', *Literature/Film Quarterly*, 21, 2, 102–11.

Waller, Gregory (1986) *The Living and the Undead: From Stoker's Dracula to Romero's Dawn of the Dead.* Urbana and Chicago: University of Illinois Press.

Warshow, Robert (1971a) 'The Gangster as Tragic Hero', in *The Immediate Experience.* New York: Atheneum, 127–34.

_____ (1971b) 'Movie Chronicle: The Westerner', in *The Immediate Experience.* New

York: Atheneum, 135–54.

Wells, Paul (2000) *The Horror Genre: From Beezlebub to Blair Witch*. London: Wallflower Press.

Williams, Alan (1984) 'Is a Radical Genre Criticism Possible?', *Quarterly Review of Film Studies*, 9, 2 (Spring), 121–5.

Williams, Linda (2003 [1991]) 'Film Bodies: Gender, Genre and Excess' in Barry Keith Grant (ed.) *Film Genre Reader 3*. Austin: University of Texas Press, 141–159.

Wood, Robin (1968) *Howard Hawks*. London: Secker & Warburg/British Film Institute.

____ (1979a) 'The American Family Comedy: From *Meet Me in St. Louis* to *The Texas Chainsaw Massacre*', *Wide Angle*, 3, 2, 5–11.

____ (1979b) 'An Introduction to the American Horror Film', in Richarrd Lippe and Robin Wood (eds) *American Nightmare: Essays on the Horror Film*. Toronto: Festival of Festivals, 7–28.

____ (1986) *Hollywood from Vietnam to Reagan*. New York: Columbia University Press.

____ (1989) *Hitchcock's Films Revisited*. New York: Columbia University Press.

____ (1996 [1983]) 'Burying the Undead: The Use and Obsolescence of Count Dracula' in Barry Keith Grant (ed.) *The Dread of Difference: Gender and the Horror Film*. Austin: University of Texas Press, 364–78.

____ (2003 [1977]) 'Ideology, Genre, Auteur', in Barry Keith Grant (ed.) *Film Genre Reader 3*. Austin: University of Texas Press, 60–74.

Wright, Judith Hess (2003 [1974]) 'Genre Films and the Status Quo', in Barry Keith Grant (ed.) *Film Genre Reader 3*. Austin: University of Texas Press, 42–50.

Wright, Will (1976) *Sixguns and Society: A Structural Study of the Western*. Berkeley: University of California Press.

INDEX

.

GPSR Authorized Representative: Easy Access System Europe, Mustamäe tee 50, 10621 Tallinn, Estonia, gpsr.requests@easproject.com

www.ingramcontent.com/pod-product-compliance
Ingram Content Group UK Ltd.
Pitfield, Milton Keynes, MK11 3LW, UK
UKHW032044140325
456291UK00002B/27